Following Jesus

What the New Testament Teaches Us

Following Jesus

What the New Testament Teaches Us

Daniel J. Harrington, S.J.

Our Sunday Visitor Publishing Division
Our Sunday Visitor, Inc.
Huntington, Indiana 46750

17 16 15 14 13 12 1 2 3 4 5 6 7 8 9

ISBN: 978-1-59276-159-3 (Inventory No. T1190)
eISBN: 978-1-61278-297-3
LCCN: 2012950886

Interior design by Sherri L. Hoffman
Cover design by Amanda Falk

Cover image: *The Calling of St. Peter*, from a series of scenes of the New Testament (fresco), Barna da Siena (fl.1350-55) / Collegiata, San Gimignano, Italy / Alinari / The Bridgeman Art Library

PRINTED IN THE UNITED STATES OF AMERICA

Contents

Introduction

In my book *Jesus the Revelation of the Father's Love: What the New Testament Teaches Us* (2010), I tried to show that the concept of Jesus as the revelation of God's love for us is the central and most basic theme of the Christian Bible. This book takes up where the former book left off. It deals with the theme of following Jesus (or discipleship), and concerns the various responses that Jesus as the revelation of the Father's love elicited both before and after his death and resurrection. Thus this book is a sequel or even a "twin" to my earlier volume.

The basic thesis of this book is that to be a disciple of Jesus is not only to become his student (the core meaning of the Greek word *mathetes* in antiquity) in an intellectual sense but also (and especially) to be so "conformed" to his person (see Philippians 3:10–11) as to "imitate" him in his self-sacrificing love for others and even take on his identity as the Son of God (in faith and baptism). However, as the New Testament shows, there is more than one way to become a follower of Jesus and more than one way to live out our Christian identity. The New Testament texts on discipleship also teach us to expect discouragement and suffering along the way, since "a disciple is not above the teacher" (Matthew 10:24). Nevertheless, these same texts also promise followers of Jesus "a hundredfold now in this age . . . and in the age to come eternal life" (Mark 10:30).

Each of the four parts of this book will deal with six key New Testament passages that develop in various ways the theme of following Jesus. The first part focuses on pertinent texts in the first three Gospels (Matthew, Mark, and Luke) and their very challenging teachings about discipleship. The second part considers how various characters in John's Gospel gradually come to a better understanding and appreciation of Jesus through their encounter with him. The third part discusses Paul the apostle of Jesus as someone so conformed to Christ that he could boast, "It is not longer I who live, but Christ who lives in me" (Galatians 2:20). The fourth part looks at some relatively minor characters in the New Testament and shows how they too can contribute to the recognition that there are many ways of being a follower of Jesus.

What follows is once more an exercise in biblical theology. In it I want to help readers enter into some key New Testament texts in their literary and historical contexts, and to suggest how their theological thoughts might illuminate and challenge us today. At the end of each of the four parts I have included a summary statement as well as some helps toward personal assimilation (THINK, PRAY, and ACT). The brief bibliography points toward books in which the theme of discipleship in the New Testament is treated in greater detail and depth than it is here.

My hope is that this book will be used not only for personal study and prayer but also in Bible study groups. I especially hope that it might increase in those who read and use it a greater appreciation of Sacred Scripture as the "soul" of Christian theology and life, and that they may come to receive the good news about Jesus proclaimed in the Bible "not as a human word but as what it really is, God's word which is also at work in you believers" (1 Thessalonians 2:13).

Once more I must thank Bert Ghezzi for suggesting this project and encouraging me along the way. It has been a pleasure to work with him again. The biblical quotations are taken from the New Revised Standard Version. This book should be used alongside a Bible.

1

HEARING

Jesus' Call in the Synoptic Gospels

In many respects the first three Gospels in the New Testament — Matthew, Mark, and Luke — share a common vision of Jesus and his first followers, and that is why they are often referred to as the Synoptic Gospels. All three Gospels divide their narratives of Jesus' public ministry into three major geographical phases: Galilee as the place where Jesus calls his first followers who then witness his wise teachings and miraculous healings; his journey from northern Galilee to Jerusalem when Jesus teaches his disciples and others about his own identity and what it means to follow him; and Jerusalem where he exercises a brief public ministry and then is arrested, is abandoned by most of his male disciples, is condemned to death, suffers various kinds of abuse, dies by crucifixion, and is said by former disciples to have been raised from the dead on Easter Sunday.

Besides Jesus who is the obvious focus of attention in these three Gospels, the disciples of Jesus, whether they are the Twelve Apostles or other followers, are next in prominence. While the

Evangelists' portraits of the disciples have much in common, they also have some distinctive emphases. Mark, writing around A.D. 70, has the disciples get off to a good start in responding generously to Jesus' call to be with him and share his mission. However, as the narrative proceeds, they become increasingly dense and obtuse, so that at the cross only the women followers remain faithful. Matthew, writing around A.D. 85 or 90, uses Mark and other sources but softens somewhat Mark's portrait in favor of presenting Peter and his companions as having only a "little faith." Luke, however, is even more positive about Jesus' first followers. He traces the pattern of discipleship back to Mary the mother of Jesus (hearing the word of God and acting upon it) and presents the apostles as representatives of continuity between the time of Jesus (Luke's Gospel) and the time of the early church and its spread throughout the Mediterranean world (Acts of the Apostles), while giving greater prominence to the women followers of Jesus (see Luke 8:1–3).

1. Mary as the First Disciple

> *"Then Mary said, 'Here I am, the servant of the Lord; let it be with me according to your word.' Then the angel departed from her."*
>
> — LUKE 1:38

As the result of serious biblical study, the description of Mary the mother of Jesus as the "first disciple" of Jesus has become popular in recent years. The idea is based mainly on Luke's Gospel, and first of all on the account of the announcement of Jesus' birth to Mary in Luke 1:26–38. That narrative places Mary's discipleship in line with several great figures in the Old Testament and points forward to the New Testament ideal of Jesus' disciple as one who strives to hear the word of God and to act upon it.

The way in which the story of the Annunciation is told in Luke 1:26–38 is reminiscent of the "call" stories about Moses in Exodus 3–4 and Gideon in Judges 6, as well as those about the prophets in Isaiah 6 and Jeremiah 1. In most cases there is a commission, an objection, a reassurance, a sign, another objection, and a final acceptance of the commission. The content of Mary's call and commission to be the mother of the Messiah and the Son of God is treated at length in *Jesus the Revelation of the Father's Love,* pp. 12–15. Here I want only to focus on Mary's response to the commission and its significance for the theme of discipleship in the New Testament.

In reading Luke 1:26–38 we are to imagine Mary as a young women living in the somewhat obscure town of Nazareth in Galilee. She is engaged to a man named Joseph. Most likely this was a match arranged by their families. When greeted by the angel Gabriel as the "favored one" (= "full of grace"), Mary is naturally puzzled. When the angel tells her that she is to become the mother of the long awaited Messiah of Israel, she is puzzled even more. And so she objects that fulfilling this commission is impossible since she is a virgin, thus suggesting that she has not had sexual intercourse and perhaps does not ever intend to do so. As the angel makes the mode of the Messiah's birth even more grandiose ("by the Holy Spirit") and the dignity of the child even greater ("Son of God"), her puzzlement grows even more. So Gabriel has to offer her some sign that such a birth might be at all possible. The sign is the surprising pregnancy of Mary's elderly relative, Elizabeth, who is to be the mother of John the Baptist. Only then does Mary leave behind her fears and doubts, and utters the remarkable response that has come to be known as her *Fiat*: (Latin for "let it be done"): "Let it be with me according to your word" (Luke 1:38). How the narrative unfolds captures Mary's very human struggle to accept the call of God and at the same time places her experience in line with great biblical figures like Moses, Gideon, Isaiah, and Jeremiah.

Mary's *Fiat* emphasizes her acceptance of God's word conveyed through the angel. That word of God is something even more current and active than the written word of Scripture. Rather, it reflects the experience of God's will made known in the depths of the human person. In the following episode known as the Visitation (Luke 1:39–45), Elizabeth blesses Mary as one "who believed that there would be a fulfillment of what was spoken to her by the Lord" (1:45). At the end of Luke's infancy narrative we are told that Jesus' mother "treasured all these things in her heart" (2:51).

When the adult Jesus comes to define discipleship in his movement, he does so in terms of family relationships and uses the language used of Mary in Luke's infancy narrative: "My mother and my brothers are those who hear the word of God and do it" (8:20). Likewise, in Luke 11:28, Jesus declares blessed "those who hear the word of God and obey it" — which is exactly what Mary does. Thus Luke adapts sayings that if taken out of context might reflect badly on Mary and casts the definition of discipleship in terms already connected with Mary.

While Luke does not explicitly mention Mary's presence at the cross of Jesus (as John 19:26–27 does), he certainly prepares for it with Simeon's prophecy in Luke 2:35: "and a sword will pierce your own soul too." And in Acts 1:14 Luke places Mary the mother of Jesus among the first followers of Jesus gathered in Jerusalem after Jesus' ascension and awaiting the descent of the Holy Spirit at Pentecost. That means that Mary is the only person who remains with Jesus from birth to death. And throughout she embodies Jesus' own ideal of a disciple as one who hears the word of God and acts upon it.

Was Mary the first disciple of Jesus? That depends on how you define being a disciple. Is it reserved for those called by the adult Jesus to follow him? However, it is fair to say that Mary's *Fiat* was integral to the process by which the Word became flesh (John 1:14). Many Catholic doctrines about Mary — the Immaculate Conception, the Virgin Birth, and the Assumption — stress aspects of Mary in which she is different from ordinary humans. So it may be helpful to take a lead from Luke and balance them with what we find out about Mary as a human person like ourselves in Luke's Gospel: her deep roots in the piety of Israel, her struggle to discern God's will for her, her generous acceptance of God's commission to be the mother of the Messiah, her fidelity to her son Jesus even in suffering, and her exemplary dedication to the task of hearing the word of God and acting upon it. Those are good grounds, I think, for describing Mary as the first disciple of Jesus.

2. Apostles Called by Jesus

> *"As Jesus passed along the Sea of Galilee, he saw Simon and his brother Andrew casting a net into the sea — for they were fishermen. And Jesus said to them, 'Follow me and I will make you fish for people.' And immediately they left their nets and followed him."*
>
> — Mark 1:16–18

Unlike the other Evangelists, Mark does not begin his story of Jesus from his conception and birth (as Matthew and Luke do) or with his existence from eternity (as John does). Rather, he begins with Jesus' public ministry in Galilee (in the northern part of the land of Israel). From the prologue in Mark 1:1–13 we learn that Jesus' coming was foreseen by the prophets, that John the Baptist looked forward to his coming, that at his baptism he was identified as the Son of God, and that he overcame testing by Satan in the wilderness. When the adult Jesus bursts on the public stage, he proclaims in Mark 1:14–15 what is an apt summary of all his teaching and healing activity: "The time is fulfilled, and the kingdom of God has come near; repent, and believe in the good news."

In Mark's version of the call of the first disciples in 1:16–20 (and Matthew 4:18–22), Jesus is walking along the shore of the Sea of Galilee and sees Simon and his brother Andrew fishing with their nets. They are professional fishermen. Then he stops, looks at them, and says, "Follow me and I will make you fish for people." Thus he is inviting them to become his disciples, and challenges them to leave behind their former profession, and to apply their energies and skills to the task of saving human persons instead of catching fish. Their response is complete and immediate. They follow him without hesitation. Then Jesus repeats the process with another set of brothers who are also fishermen — James and John, the sons of Zebedee. When Jesus calls, they too follow immediately, leaving behind their father with his hired men in the boat.

As attractive as this story may be, it does raise two important questions: What did the first disciples leave behind? And why did they do it? Jesus encounters these first four followers as they are engaged in their work as fishermen. The fact that they have nets and boats means that they were professional fishermen, not lazy men wasting time on a sunny afternoon.

Thus they were leaving behind a stable source of income, since the Sea of Galilee has long been a prime fishing ground. The first followers were basically small businessmen. And they were also leaving behind their families. James and John left their father Zebedee. And from Mark 1:30 we learn that Peter had a mother-in-law nearby, and presumably a wife (unless he was by then a widower; but see 1 Corinthians 9:5).

Why did they leave? The Markan and Matthean accounts of Jesus' call of the first disciples suggest that there had been no prior contact between them. Compare Luke 5:1–11 and John 1:29–42, which presuppose some contact through a miraculous catch of fish or through the witness of John the Baptist. In Mark and Matthew, however, Jesus appears on the scene, says, "Follow me," and these fishermen do so. The very lack of prior contact forces the reader to ask, why did they accept Jesus' invitation "immediately"?

One way to explain it is to appeal to the overwhelming attractiveness of Jesus. That is, his person and word were so powerful as to move grown men to leave behind their families and their businesses in order to follow an itinerant preacher whom they had not known only on the strength of his command, "Follow me." Thus the scene constitutes Mark's initial effort at implicit Christology. The absence of obvious motivation generates the question in the reader, "Who is this Jesus of Nazareth," that he could evoke such a response?

Another approach links the story of the call of the first disciples to the summary of Jesus' preaching about the kingdom of God in Mark 1:15. It is entirely possible that these fishermen shared the hopes of many of their Jewish contemporaries for God's definitive display of power and sovereignty over creation. Perhaps they too were already praying, "Thy kingdom come!" And when Jesus came along, they intuited that in him those hopes might be fulfilled. Indeed, those hopes were fulfilled, but probably not in the way they imagined as they set out on the path of discipleship.

As the first disciples begin to accompany Jesus in Mark's narrative, they witness displays of his miraculous healing power and of his wisdom as a teacher who is able to escape the traps set by his opponents. When Jesus decides to constitute the twelve apostles as the inner circle of his movement, the first disciples head the list: "Simon (to whom he gave the name Peter); James son of Zebedee and John the brother of James (to whom he gave the name Boanerges, that is, Sons of Thunder); and Andrew" (Mark 3:17–18). The apostles' job description appears in Mark 3:14–15: "and he appointed twelve, whom he also named apostles, to be with him, and to be sent out to proclaim the message, and to have authority to cast out demons." The essence of discipleship in Jesus' movement is being with Jesus, and sharing in his mission. This remains the best description of Christian discipleship that I know.

However, as the first disciples witness Jesus' wise teachings about the kingdom of God and his powerful actions, they still do not understand him adequately. In Mark's view, they have to be exposed to the mystery of the cross and to Jesus' identity as a suffering Messiah. Their failure reaches the point at the end of Jesus' public ministry in Galilee (Mark 8:14–21) that Jesus batters them with seven pointed questions that amount to what we find in 8:17, "Do you still not perceive or understand?"

At the center of Mark's narrative is the journey of Jesus and his disciples from northern Galilee to Jerusalem in 8:22 to 10:52. The journey is bracketed by healings of two blind men, one who comes to see only gradually (8:22–26), and the other (Bartimaeus) who comes to see immediately and follows Jesus along the "way" of discipleship (10:46–52). In their present position these stories have obvious symbolic and theological value. Along the way, Peter correctly identifies Jesus as the Messiah (8:29). But when Jesus forecasts his own passion and death (and resurrection) three times (8:31; 9:31; 10:33–34), the disciples misunderstand him at every point and seem more interested in calculating their own relative importance in the coming kingdom.

During Jesus' ministry in Jerusalem, his first followers do not show themselves much better at understanding Jesus or acting courageously in his service. One of them, Judas Iscariot, enters into a plot with the chief priests to betray Jesus. The others ignore or resist his warnings about his impending suffering. Some fall asleep during his prayer in Gethsemane, and scatter at his arrest. And Peter denies three times even knowing Jesus.

Only the women followers remain faithful, even if "from a distance." But Mark has never mentioned them before the scene at the cross in 15:40–41. Now he names them: "Mary Magdalene, and Mary the mother of James the younger and of Joses, and Salome." Only now does he tell us that "they used to follow him and provided for him when he was in Galilee." And now he adds that "there were many other women who had come up with him to Jerusalem." The principle of continuity is Mary Magdalene. She was with Jesus along the way; she sees Jesus die; she sees where he is buried; and she finds his tomb empty on Easter Sunday morning.

What does Mark's narrative tell us about following Jesus? The first disciples start well enough. They accept Jesus' call "Follow me" immediately and generously. They illustrate well what discipleship is: being with Jesus, and sharing in his mission. They listen to his teaching and observe his miracles. Their problems seem to arise from a refusal to grasp what it means to follow Jesus the suffering Messiah. They seem to expect Jesus to be a nationalistic military and political messiah, not one who suffers and dies. When faced with that prospect, they want to change the topic and speculate about their own future glory. They become negative examples, who serve to highlight the fidelity and nobility of Jesus. Only when they (and we as Mark's readers) confront the mystery of the cross, can they (and we) correctly perceive Jesus the suffering Messiah and really follow him. That remains the real challenge facing all prospective disciples of Jesus: to embrace the mystery of the cross.

3. Apostles Sent on a Mission

> *"As you go, proclaim the good news, 'The kingdom of heaven has come near.' Cure the sick, raise the dead, cleanse the lepers, cast out demons. You received without payment; give without payment."*
>
> — Matthew 10:7–8

In Matthew's Gospel there are five extended speeches or discourses by Jesus. The most famous of these is the Sermon on the Mount in chapters 5 through 7. That great sermon is followed by a series of ten or so miracle stories interspersed with sayings about discipleship in chapters 8–9. The point is that Jesus is powerful both in word and deed. Then at the end of chapter 9 and all through chapter 10 Jesus gives what is called the Missionary Discourse. This speech spells out what it means for disciples to share in the mission of Jesus. The discourse concerns the goal of the mission (preparation for the coming kingdom of God), the means for carrying it out (itinerant preaching), and the circumstances under which it is carried out (including danger).

Missionary discourses are prominent features in all three Synoptic Gospels. In Mark's Gospel there is a short missionary discourse placed in 6:6b–13, after the rejection of Jesus in Nazareth and before the account of John the Baptist's death. In Luke's Gospel there are two missionary discourses, a short one directed to the Twelve Apostles (9:1–6), and a longer one in 10:1–16 directed to the wider circle of Seventy (or Seventy-two) other disciples. Matthew has taken over material from Mark and greatly expanded the Missionary Discourse to cover all of chapter 10 (more precisely, 9:35–11:1). These discourses give practical advice about disciples sharing in Jesus' mission of teaching and healing, and what can be expected by and from those who do so. While many of the details most obviously pertain to conditions in first-century Israel/Palestine, the inclusion of these texts in the Synoptic Gospels suggests that they have a much wider significance, and that their basic principles can be applied in many different times and places.

In the Mediterranean world of the first century (including Palestine), philosophies and religions were promoted mainly by traveling "missionaries" who went from place to place. Some depended on friends for support and lodging, while others had to rely on the kindness of strangers. In the age before printing or electronic media, the principal means of promoting one's teachings or beliefs was through the spoken word. This might involve "street-corner" preaching, an invitation to address an existing group (such as a synagogue or some other voluntary association), or permission to provide entertainment and/or distraction for manual workers (Paul and the tentmakers/

leather workers). It was an oral culture, and missionaries had to work hard to persuade others of their wisdom by their rhetorical skill. Of course, there were also a fair number of charlatans trying to fool people into giving them money and other valuables (including prestige). And conversely, an effective way to gain new followers was to charge one's rivals with being in it only for the money or the prestige. This was the world into which Jesus sent his apostles and other disciples.

The Matthean disciples of Jesus have the advantage of being exposed already to Jesus' Sermon on the Mount in Matthew 5–7. From it they know about the values and attitudes prized and exemplified by Jesus, the social significance of being his disciples (salt of the earth, light of the world), and his program of fulfilling (and not abolishing) the Law and the Prophets by going to the root of matters. They also know that acts of piety should be carried out to please God (and not to gain honor and a good reputation before others), that in all areas of life they should act wisely and righteously, and that they possess a solid foundation for their lives in the teachings of Jesus.

The fullest missionary discourse in the Gospels appears in Matthew 10. After summarizing Jesus' activity of preaching and healing in Matthew 9:35 (see 4:23), we are given two reasons why Jesus wanted to expand his mission: because the people of Israel were like sheep without a shepherd (they had no adequate spiritual leadership), and because there were not enough workers to bring in the harvest (a biblical symbol of the kingdom of God). And so he commissions his Twelve Apostles to carry on his work as teacher and healer. The list of their names is headed by the first disciples he called (Simon and Andrew, James and John), and includes Judas Iscariot ("the one who betrayed him") at the end.

The first part of Jesus' discourse (Matthew 10:5–15) confines the apostles' mission to Israel. Only after Jesus' resurrection they will be sent to "all nations" (Matthew 28:19). Their message is to be the message of John the Baptist (3:2) and Jesus (4:17): "The kingdom of heaven has come near." They are to do what Jesus did according to Matthew 10:8–9: "Cure the sick, raise the dead, cleanse the lepers, cast out demons." They are not to accept payment, and are to travel light ("no gold or silver or copper . . . no bag or two tunics or sandals"), trusting in God and relying on the hospitality of strangers. The simplicity of their lifestyle will be evidence of the authenticity of their mission. They are also warned against wasting time and energy in trying to find better accommodations, and are told to expect rejection. In the face of rejection and hostility, they are counseled to leave whatever retaliation there may be to God.

The second part (10:16–25) develops further the theme of the cost of discipleship. Jesus first warns the apostles that they will find themselves as sheep in the midst of wolves, and that they should be wise as serpents and innocent as doves. The danger of their situation is emphasized in 10:17–18 (public trials) and in 10:21–22 (family conflicts), but is mitigated by promises of divine help in 10:19–20 (from the Holy Spirit) and 10:23 (the coming of the Son of Man). By way of summary, Jesus reminds them that they can expect to share the fate of their teacher Jesus. And so some people will charge that they are really agents of Beelzebul (= Satan), and not of the Holy Spirit (see 12:22–32).

The third part (10:26–42) treats various topics pertaining to discipleship and its dangers. Prospective disciples must trust in God's loving care for them, and they should fear only those who can destroy their souls (10:26–31). On their willingness (or unwillingness) to confess Jesus publicly they will judged by their heavenly Father (10:32–33). They must be prepared for family divisions as a result of their commitment to Jesus, and be willing to place it above their obligations to blood relatives (10:34–39). Finally according to 10:40–42, they must welcome all kinds of persons, no matter how important or insignificant they might seem to be, as they would welcome Jesus and the one who sent him (his Father). Matthew's Missionary Discourse ends as do the other major discourses in his Gospel (see 7:28; 13:53; 19:1; 26:1), with the phrase "Now when Jesus had finished . . ." (11:1).

Despite its original setting in first-century Palestine/Israel, Matthew's Missionary Discourse contains some enduring values pertaining to his followers' participation in his mission of proclaiming God's kingdom and bringing healing to those in need. Jesus' disciples must live against the horizon of hope for the full coming of God's kingdom even as they also proclaim its present dimensions. Their mission is in this world and involves the hopes and fears of people in spiritual and physical need. Sharing in Jesus' mission demands letting go of material attachments (money, ease, prestige, etc.) in the service of that mission, which has become the most important thing in life. When encountering resistance, rejection, and hostility, the response of Jesus' disciples must be nonviolent, leaving the final verdict to God's judgment. Jesus' followers must expect suffering after the pattern of their teacher, Jesus. They must let go of their fears and grow in trust with regard to God and God's future. They must be willing to confess Jesus publicly as Lord. Their loyalty to God must even override their attachments and obligations to their families. And they must try to see in every person, especially the "little ones," the image of Christ and his Father.

4. The Cost of Discipleship

> *"Whoever does not carry the cross and follow me cannot be my disciple."*
>
> — Luke 14:27

In the late 1930s, Dietrich Bonhoeffer, who was then the most promising young Protestant theologian in Germany, wrote a book whose English title is *The Cost of Discipleship.* Several years afterward he was arrested and executed for resisting Hitler and the Nazi movement in April 1945. For Bonhoeffer, discipleship — fidelity to the gospel and to Christian principles — had a very high cost. His experience has been repeated many times before and since, for example, by the Jesuit Ignacio Ellacuria and his companions in El Salvador, in 1989.

Jesus' short discourse in Luke 14:25–33 concerns the high cost of discipleship and the need to count that cost. (For an earlier, pre-journey reflection on the cost of discipleship, see the various sayings about taking up the cross and related matters in Luke 9:23–26.) This discourse occurs on the way, roughly in the middle of Jesus' final journey to Jerusalem, where the major topics are the identity of Jesus (Christology) and what it means to follow him (discipleship). It is addressed to the "large crowds" who were traveling with him. It consists of three "hard" sayings and two short parables.

The first hard saying (Luke 14:26) — about "hating" one's family — places before the prospective disciple the choice between following Jesus (in the sense of joining his immediate circle) and observing the traditional family ties and obligations. This was an even more difficult choice in first-century Palestine than it may be for most people in twenty-first-century America. The term "hate" in the saying, while an obvious exaggeration, underlines the overriding importance of God's kingdom and following Jesus in comparison with even the most sacred human obligations.

The second hard saying (14:27) — about taking up the cross — asserts that following Jesus can and will involve suffering. Since it may well have a high cost, those who decide to follow Jesus must be prepared to take up the cross. Here the cross is to be understood as not only an instrument of physical torment but also as an occasion of public shame. The challenge to the prospective disciple involves being willing to imitate Jesus' example of suffering for the sake of the kingdom of God and in fidelity to the Father of our Lord Jesus Christ.

The hard sayings are interrupted by two short parables about counting the cost of discipleship. The first parable (14:28–30) concerns a man who contemplates building a tower. Unless he carefully plans out the project and calculates the cost, he will not be able to finish it and will be exposed as a fool before his neighbors.

Similarly, according to the parable in 14:31–32, a king who wants to go to war must take account of the strength and resources of his own army and what resistance he can expect from his enemies. Otherwise he will have to beg for a peace treaty and suffer shame before both his opponents and his own troops. The point of these two parables is that we must recognize beforehand the high cost that discipleship may exact from us before we make the commitment, and then we must do all we can to fulfill that commitment.

The third hard saying (14:33) concerns the willingness to renounce material possessions to follow Jesus. This challenge would also have been very difficult in Jesus' time. In some circles (then as now) having many possessions was interpreted as both a blessing from God and a sign of one's personal cleverness and goodness. Moreover, there was no welfare state or social safety net beyond the family to provide for the basic necessities of human life. And the social and religious ideal was to be a rich person who could then serve as a benefactor to those in need, and thus develop a reputation for being the "great man" as Job had been before his downfall (see Job 29). Again the extreme nature of the challenge to forgo developing a good social and religious profile, providing security for oneself and one's family, and acting as a public benefactor highlights the overriding importance of God's kingdom and following Jesus on the way to it.

The account of the rich ruler in Luke 18:18–23 (see Mark 10:17–22; Matthew 19:16–22) illustrates concretely the difficulty involved in responding to accepting the challenge of the third hard saying. When the man approaches Jesus to learn what he needs to do to "inherit eternal life," Jesus lists several of the Ten Commandments. When the man says that he has observed them since he was a young man, Jesus challenges him to sell all that he has, distribute the proceeds to the poor, and follow him as a disciple. That meant forgoing the privileges that come with wealth and being a benefactor in favor of direct fellowship with Jesus, something that the "rich ruler" felt was too costly to do.

Nevertheless, after commenting on the danger of possessing riches (because we make them into idols) as a possible obstacle to entering the kingdom of God, Jesus in Luke 18:29–30 promises those who do follow him as disciples "very much more in this age, and in the age to come eternal life."

While following Jesus may have high costs, what makes discipleship possible is the grace of God and the hope of eternal life with God. We are not alone as we accompany Jesus and move forward toward the fullness of life in God's kingdom. Indeed as with the first disciples, he has taken the initiative in calling us to be his followers. We can and will deal with the cost of discipleship, as Bonhoeffer and Ellacuria did, if we are truly convinced that God is with us, calling, directing, and helping us along the way.

5. Peter's "Little Faith"

> *"Jesus immediately reached out his hand and caught him, saying to him, 'You of little faith, why did you doubt?'"*
>
> — MATTHEW 14:31

As we have seen, Simon Peter was among the first of those called to be disciples by Jesus (Mark 1:16–20; Matthew 4:18–22), and is always named first on the various lists of the Twelve Apostles (Mark 3:16; Matthew 10:2; Luke 6:14; Acts 1:13). The narratives about him in Acts and the letters known as 1 and 2 Peter, as well as references to him in Paul's letters (Galatians 1:18; 2:11; etc.), indicate that he remained an important figure in early Christian circles.

The Evangelist Matthew shows a special interest in Peter. While including much material about Peter from Mark's Gospel, he presents Peter as a disciple who struggles and wavers to be faithful to Jesus. Even though Peter wholeheartedly accepts the challenge of following Jesus, his response remains imperfect until his experience of the risen Jesus. Matthew's characteristic phrase for Peter and the other disciples during Jesus' earthly ministry is "little faith."

The phrase "little faith" is not as bad as it may sound on first hearing. As we have seen, Mark portrays the disciples as making a good beginning by generously accepting Jesus' call and fulfilling the ideal of being with Jesus and sharing in his mission. However, just before their journey to Jerusalem (Mark 8:21), Jesus rebukes them with the question, "Do you not yet understand?" What they have to come to understand is that Jesus is a suffering Messiah, and that the mystery of the cross is the means by which a new and better relationship with God has been made possible. Along the way they all too often fail to understand Jesus and end up fleeing him and even denying him in the passion narrative. Matthew, however, seems to want to upgrade the image of Peter and the Apostles. He does so paradoxically with the concept of "little faith."

Matthew believes that "little faith" is better than none at all. The application of the concept to Peter comes to the fore in the episode of Jesus walking on the water in Matthew 14:22–33. Matthew took over most of this episode from Mark 6:45–52. Having sent the disciples to go by boat to the other side of the Sea of Galilee, Jesus goes to a mountain to pray. However, during the night a storm comes up, and the disciples begin to struggle in their boat. At dawn they see Jesus walking on the water and coming in their direction. To quiet their fears Jesus reassures them, "Take heart, it is I; do not be afraid" (14:27). In walking on the water, Jesus does what God does according to Job 9:8. When the storm calms down and Jesus gets into the boat, the disciples acknowledge Jesus as "the Son of God" (14:33).

Between Jesus' words in 14:27 and the resolution of the crisis in 14:32–33, there is an episode in 14:28–31 that features Peter and appears only in Matthew's Gospel. The impulsive Peter seeks to verify that Jesus really is the one walking on the water, and asks, "Lord, if it is you, command me to come to you on the water." When Jesus agrees, Peter gets out of the boat, and starts walking on the water too. However, he soon gets frightened by a strong wind, starts to sink, and cries out, "Lord, save me!" On rescuing Peter from drowning, Jesus summarizes the episode with the question, "You of little faith, why did you doubt?"

Thus Peter in 14:28–31 becomes the perfect illustration of "little faith" He starts well enough. But when things get tough, he loses confidence and flounders on being left to his own devices. While the theme of "little faith" appears earlier in the part of the Sermon on the Mount about trusting in God's providential care (6:30) and in the stilling of the storm (8:26), it is especially prominent in chapters 14–18, where Peter and the other disciples are major figures. Their little faith contrasts with the "unbelief" shown in the synagogue at Nazareth (13:58) and the perfect trust in his heavenly Father displayed by Jesus throughout the Gospel. In 16:8 Matthew tempers Jesus' scathing criticism of the Twelve in Mark 8:14–21 by characterizing them as "you of little faith." And in 17:20 he explains the disciples' inability to heal the epileptic boy in terms of their own "little faith."

In Matthew 14–18 Peter is the one who gets involved as the spokesman when special problems arise. In 15:15 he asks for an explanation from Jesus about the observance of Jewish food regulations. In 16:16 he speaks on behalf of the other disciples and identifies Jesus as "the Messiah, the Son of the living God." In 17:24–27 he brings to Jesus' attention the dispute about paying the temple tax. And in 18:21–22 he asks Jesus for a clarification about how many times his followers might be expected to forgive one another. But in 16:23 he is rebuked by Jesus for refusing to accept his first passion prediction, and in 26:69–75 he denies even knowing Jesus three times.

Thus Matthew portrays Peter with some ambivalence. He is among the first followers of Jesus, is the most prominent among the Twelve Apostles, and serves as their representative at various points. And yet Peter also has a dark side that causes him at times to lose trust and even deny Jesus. However, the most important episode about Peter in Matthew's Gospel comes in 16:17–19. Here Peter appears at his most positive. On his identifying Jesus as "the Messiah, the Son of the living God," Jesus praises Peter as the recipient of a divine revelation, and promises that he will build his church "on this rock" (a play on the words for "rock" in Aramaic [*kepha*] and in Greek [*petra*] and Peter's name [*Cephas*] in Aramaic and [*Petros*] in Greek). He also promises to give him the keys of the kingdom of heaven and the power to bind and loose on earth. However, the mood changes rapidly in 16:21–23 when Peter balks at accepting Jesus as a suffering Messiah, and Jesus dismisses him as a "Satan" (a tempter as in Job 1–2) and as being concerned more with human matters than with divine matters.

Try as he might to be a faithful follower of Jesus, the Matthean Peter often falls short of the ideal of discipleship. Indeed, he is the perfect example of "little faith." We have to wait for the time after Jesus' resurrection for the real Peter — the fearless preacher of the good news about Jesus — to appear in the Acts of the Apostles. In the meantime, Peter and the other disciples in the Gospels who display "little faith" have been sources of consolation for fallible followers of Jesus throughout the centuries.

6. Recognizing the Risen Jesus

> *"They said to each other, 'Were not our hearts burning within us while he was talking to us on the road, while he was opening the scriptures to us?'"*
>
> — LUKE 24:32

The appearance of the risen Jesus to two disciples on the road to Emmaus in Luke 24:13–35 has been described as everyone's favorite Easter story. It concerns two discouraged followers of Jesus on Easter Sunday afternoon. It also features a mysterious stranger who accompanies them on the road and turns out to be the risen Jesus. The two followers move from disappointment ("we had hoped") to burning hearts and shouts of joy. For them and for other early followers of Jesus, Easter changed everything.

In the Gospels there are two types of Easter stories. Each Gospel has its own version of the "opened" or "empty" tomb of Jesus discovered by Mary Magdalene and witnessed by other disciples (Mark 16:1–8; Matthew 28:1–8; Luke 24:1–10; John 20:1–10). Of itself, the empty tomb account proves only that Jesus' tomb was found opened, and his corpse was not there.

More important and persuasive for Easter faith are the many accounts of appearances by the risen Jesus to persons who had been his followers before his death and resurrection. They knew who Jesus was; they knew that he had died; they knew where he was buried; and now they experienced him as alive again. For the earliest list of witnesses, see 1 Corinthians 15:5–8. In Matthew 28 there are appearances in Jerusalem to Mary Magdalene and the other women (28:9–10) and in Galilee to the eleven disciples (28:16–20). In John's Gospel there are appearances first in Jerusalem to Mary Magdalene (20:11–18), to the disciples apart from Thomas (20:19–23), and to the disciples including Thomas (20:24–29). Then in John 21 there are appearances in Galilee to seven disciples, Peter, and the Beloved Disciple. The two major appearance stories in Luke 24:13–35 and 24:36–49 take place in Jerusalem and environs, and explain how Jesus' followers came to recognize him in his risen state. In both cases the recognition comes through reflection on the Old Testament Scriptures and sharing a meal. The longer ending of Mark's Gospel (16:9–20) is generally regarded as a second-century summary of the appearances recounted in the other three Gospels.

Perhaps most persuasive of all the "proofs" for Jesus' resurrection is the remarkable change that came over Jesus' followers after his resurrection. Convinced that Jesus had really been restored to life, Peter and other disciples became fearless preachers of the identity of Jesus ("Lord Jesus Christ") and what his life, death, and resurrection had achieved. Those who once deserted Jesus and even denied knowing him (Peter) now devoted their talents and energies to proclaiming that through his death and resurrection Jesus had made possible a new and better way of relating to God.

The narrative begins in Luke 24:13–16 with two disciples, Clopas and companion (not members of the Twelve), on their way from Jerusalem to Emmaus (a village in Judea whose exact location remains disputed). There they encounter the risen Jesus but fail to identify him as such. In 24:17–24 they converse with the mysterious stranger and explain why they had become so discouraged. They had hoped that Jesus was going to be "the prophet," and that he was going to restore Israel to what they imagined was its rightful (exalted) place in the world. However, they had seen him condemned and crucified by the chief priests and leaders of their people. To add to their disappointment and confusion his body had disappeared from the tomb, and they naturally assumed that it had been stolen and desecrated.

In 24:25–27, however, the mysterious stranger claims that Jesus' suffering and death were fully in accord with God's will made known in Israel's Scriptures (probably texts such as Isaiah

53 and Psalm 22), and that it was therefore necessary for the Messiah to suffer before entering into his glory. Then in 24:28–32 the mysterious stranger shares a meal with the two discouraged disciples. When he acts in ways that remind them of the feeding of the 5,000 (9:16) and the Last Supper (22:19), their eyes are opened and they recognize the mysterious stranger to be the risen Jesus. Finally in 24:33–35 the two disciples return to Jerusalem and share their good news that Jesus is alive again at a common meal with the eleven apostles (minus Judas), who repeat their experience in reverse order — coming to recognize the risen Jesus in the meal and in the Scriptures. These two episodes in Luke 24 show how encounters with the risen Christ changed everything for the first followers of Jesus, and made them into joyful and confident heralds of the good news about Jesus.

Bringing the Texts Together

The Synoptic Gospels are the most obvious resources for understanding the theme of discipleship in the New Testament. Next to Jesus, the disciples are the most prominent characters. Each Evangelist treats them as, in some respects, positive models for our admiration and imitation, and in other respects as negative examples to be avoided. What is pivotal for them all is confronting the cross and resurrection, that is, the paschal mystery, for themselves and in their own lives.

The great biblical pattern of the call to discipleship so prominent in the Old Testament can be discerned in Mary's call to become the mother of the Messiah in Luke 1. She appears as a person who fulfills the Lukan ideal of the disciple as one who seeks to grasp the word of God expressing God's will for her and to act upon it. Mark's account of the call of the first disciples in 1:16–20 indicates the attractiveness of Jesus as the one who calls and the immediate commitment that he engendered. Mark also defines discipleship as being with Jesus and sharing in his mission, while showing that even well-intentioned followers of Jesus can fail to confront properly the mystery of the cross.

The Missionary Discourse in Matthew 10 specifies the ultimate goal of the disciples' mission (preparing people for the coming kingdom of God), how the mission is to be carried out (by traveling about and proclaiming the gospel, with minimal concern for personal comfort), and the circumstances of mission (possible danger, hostility, and misunderstanding). The high cost of following Jesus and the need to count that cost are treated in Jesus' short discourse to the crowds in Luke 14:25–33 and in the episode of the rich ruler (Luke 18:18–23). However, God's grace, the value of fellowship with Jesus, and the promise of the new family of Jesus can and do outweigh the possible high costs.

The example of Peter and his "little faith" in Matthew's Gospel shows that even those closest to Jesus needed to learn the more perfect faith that comes with confronting the reality of Jesus as the suffering Messiah and the saving significance of his death and resurrection. The experience of the two discouraged disciples on the road to Emmaus in Luke 24 illustrates how their encounter with the risen Jesus changed everything, and how that encounter may be prolonged and repeated in reading the Scriptures and sharing in the Eucharistic meal.

THINK, PRAY, AND ACT

THINK

1. What do you think about the idea of Mary as the first disciple of Jesus?
2. How do you interpret the disciples' failings in Mark and Peter's "little faith" in Matthew?
3. To what extent did Jesus' resurrection transform the first followers of Jesus and reorient their discipleship?

PRAY

Read in a slow and meditative manner the other missionary discourses (besides Matthew 10) in Mark 6:7–13 and in Luke 9:1–6 and 10:1–16. What impresses you most strongly? What frightens you?

Ask God for the freedom and courage to follow Jesus in the way of discipleship, wherever it may lead you.

ACT

From the missionary discourses, take an inventory (a list of pluses and minuses) of your life thus far, and rate the quality of your own efforts at Christian discipleship.

2

GROWING in Appreciation of Jesus in John's Gospel

John's Gospel differs from the other Gospels in many respects. The public ministry of Jesus is spread over three years instead of one. During it he makes several journeys to Jerusalem rather than one. He offers long discourses rather than short packets of teaching. His healing and nature miracles are presented as "signs" that demand explanation and provide occasions for Jesus to reveal more about his person and mission. And we meet a different cast of disciples such as Nathanael, Nicodemus, the Samaritan woman, the man born blind, Lazarus and his sisters, and the mysterious figures known as the Beloved Disciple and the apostle Thomas.

In contrast to the abrupt "call" stories in the Synoptic Gospels where the discipleship narratives are so short that we can hardly understand how and why these persons would have followed Jesus at all, the discipleship stories in John's Gospel provide a more gradual approach to becoming a follower of Jesus. The initial attitudes that the prospective Johannine disciples bring to Jesus are varied: scorn, curiosity, puzzlement, blindness, disappointment, and confusion. However, under Jesus' tutelage they undergo a kind of process (mystagogy) that helps them grow in appreciating Jesus as the revealer and the revelation of God (which is the main theme of John's Gospel). This gradual approach is probably more like the way most of us have come to understand ourselves as disciples of Jesus.

1. Nathanael: From Scorn to Confession of Faith

> *"Nathanael said to him, 'Can anything good come out of Nazareth?'"*
>
> — JOHN 1:49

John's Gospel is famous for what is called its "Prologue" in chapter 1:1–18. In literature a prologue often serves to identify themes and characters to be developed in the rest of the book. The Johannine Prologue may well have originated as an early Christian hymn celebrating Jesus as the Word or Wisdom of God. It had precedents in the descriptions of Wisdom personified in Proverbs 8 and Sirach 24. It describes Jesus' existence before creation and his incarnation ("the Word became flesh and lived among us") in human history. Its use as the Gospel reading on Christmas Day enables us to capture the awesome significance of what and who the church celebrates on that day.

While John 1:1–18 deserves the title of Prologue, in fact the whole of chapter 1 functions as a prologue to the Gospel. It provides a kind of anthology of titles that are appropriately applied to Jesus. When in 1:19–28 John the Baptist refuses the titles of Messiah, Elijah, and the prophet for himself, the implication is that Jesus is in fact all of these things. In 1:29–34 John testifies that Jesus is the Lamb of God and the Son of God. The first followers of Jesus in 1:35–42 recognize him not only as the Rabbi/Teacher but also the Messiah. And in 1:43–51 Nathanael comes to recognize Jesus as both the Son of God and the King of Israel, only to be told by Jesus that he is also the glorious Son of Man. By gathering all these honorific titles at the beginning of the Gospel, John provides us as readers with important information as to who Jesus really is. And so as John proceeds to tell his story of Jesus' public life, we will know that the major figure Jesus is more than simply a sage or prophet or wonder worker.

We know little about the disciple of Jesus named Nathanael. According to John 21:2, he was from Cana in Galilee, the site of Jesus' first miracle narrated in John 2:1–11. Perhaps he was a fisherman, since he joined the others in their fishing expedition in John 21. His name does not appear in the various lists of the Twelve Apostles in the Synoptic Gospels and Acts, though tradition has equated him with Bartholomew.

The episode in John 1:43–51 that features Nathanael takes place in Galilee. There Jesus finds Philip from Bethsaida (the hometown of Andrew and Peter) and (as in the call stories in Mark and Matthew) simply says, "Follow me" and Philip does so. Philip in turn finds Nathanael, and identifies Jesus the son of Joseph of Nazareth as the one to whom Moses and the Prophets had been pointing (presumably the Messiah). Nathanael seems more concerned about the place name Nazareth than anything else. Indeed he greets the place name with scorn, "Can anything good come out of Nazareth?" (Cana was no metropolis either.)

Yet Nathanael changes his mind as well as his tone suddenly and radically when he encounters Jesus personally. When Jesus describes him as "an Israelite in whom there is no deceit," and says that he saw Nathanael under a fig tree before

Philip called him, Nathanael is stunned and addresses Jesus as "Rabbi" (an honorific title meaning "my great one" and applied to distinguished Jewish teachers), and confesses Jesus to be the Son of God and the King of Israel.

What led Nathanael to drop his scornful attitude toward Jesus and his hometown? What led him to confess Jesus to be not only the Messiah but also the Son of God? As with the call of the first disciples in Mark 1:16–20 and Matthew 4:18–22, the sudden shift in attitude seems to point toward the overwhelming attraction of the person of Jesus that could make people suddenly give up their old way of life to follow him on the way of discipleship.

Whatever Nathanael saw in Jesus, he is assured by Jesus that he will "see greater things than these." Here Jesus alludes to the story of Jacob's dream about a ladder in Genesis 28:12 bridging heaven and earth. Here Son of Man is the glorious title that identifies Jesus as the bridge or mediator between heaven and earth, between God and humankind. Thus the Nathanael episode adds Son of Man to the collection of honorific titles applied to Jesus in John 1:1–51. It also adds to our amazement regarding the power of Jesus to attract disciples by reason mainly of his personal presence and command. The major theme of John's Gospel is that Jesus is both the revealer and the revelation of God. We can only imagine how brightly that identity shone through to those first disciples whom he called to follow him.

2. Nicodemus: From Darkness to Light

> *"Now there was a Pharisee named Nicodemus, a leader of the Jews. He came to Jesus by night."*
>
> — JOHN 3:1–21

Nicodemus comes to Jesus by night. He does so presumably because as a Pharisee he does not want to be identified as a disciple of Jesus in public. At this point he is more a curious religious seeker than a committed follower of Jesus. He is a Pharisee, a member of a Jewish religious movement dedicated to interpreting and observing the Jewish Law. Although the Gospels portray the Pharisees as opponents of Jesus and often hostile toward him, of all the Jewish groups of the time Jesus probably had most in common with them and even shared an agenda with them. But sometimes "family" quarrels are the most difficult, and so Nicodemus might have been risking his place in the Pharisee movement by visiting Jesus openly and inquiring about his teachings.

What seems to have attracted Nicodemus' attention to Jesus was Jesus' ability to perform "signs." That is the usual Johannine word for the miracles as well as other extraordinary actions performed by Jesus. Thus far in John's narrative Jesus had changed water into wine at the wedding feast of Cana and performed the symbolic action of "cleansing" the Jerusalem Temple. However, from John 2:23 we learn that "when he was in Jerusalem during the Passover festival many believed in his name because they saw the signs that he was doing." Jesus, however, seems skeptical about the kind of faith built only on "signs." This explains his rather initially cool attitude toward Nicodemus. He comes to Jesus by night out of curiosity about the "signs," on the grounds that "no one can do these signs that you do apart from the presence of God."

In John 3:1–10 we are treated to a dialogue between Nicodemus and Jesus. When Nicodemus notes that Jesus must be from God (otherwise he could not do such signs), Jesus answers somewhat mysteriously that "no one can see the kingdom of

God without being born from above." Nicodemus takes the Greek adverb *anothen* to mean "again" rather than "from above" (that is, from God). Nicodemus in turn wonders how anyone can be born "again." Jesus responds that he is talking about birth from the Holy Spirit, that is, recognizing Jesus as the revelation and revealer of God, and living in accord with the promptings of the Holy Spirit.

The dialogue with Nicodemus revolves around the typical Johannine device of misunderstanding. In it Jesus makes a statement, but it is misunderstood by his interlocutor. This in turn provides the occasion for Jesus to correct the misunderstanding and to offer even more profound teachings about himself, his heavenly Father, and the kingdom of God. When in John 3:9–10 Nicodemus declares himself still puzzled ("How can these things be?"), Jesus marvels that such a teacher can fail to understand him.

The impasse created by the dialogue is broken in John 3:11–21 by a monologue that summarizes many of the key themes developed by the Johannine Jesus. Now the speaker seems to be the Johannine community rather than Jesus himself, since there is a lot of "we" language and much talk *about* Jesus. The implication is that through these teachings Nicodemus will be able to move from darkness (the night) to the light of faith.

The monologue begins in 3:11–12 with the key Johannine verbs "know" and "testify," and distinguishes between "earthly things" and "heavenly things." Next in 3:13 it identifies Jesus as "the man from heaven," the glorious Son of Man who has descended from heaven in the incarnation (John 1:14), and so is now the only one capable of teaching about "heavenly things" while on earth. In 3:14–15 it compares the "lifting up" of the Son of Man to the bronze serpent lifted up by Moses according to Numbers 21:8–9 that brought healing to the Israelites wandering in the wilderness. The verb "lift up" is a typical Johannine way of referring to the whole complex of events including Jesus' passion, death, resurrection, and exaltation/ascension. What seemed like a defeat (Jesus being lifted up on the cross) was in fact an exaltation (being lifted up to his heavenly Father). It promises that those who believe in Jesus will have "eternal life." In John's theology eternal life begins not at the time of one's death, but rather when one comes to believe in Jesus as the revealer and revelation of God.

The monologue reaches a climax with the famous saying in John 3:16, "For God so loved the world that he gave his only Son, so that everyone who believes in him may not perish but may have eternal life." In other words, the incarnation and exaltation of Jesus was a sign of God's love for humankind, and the way by which those who come to believe in Jesus may come to enjoy eternal life. In that sense Jesus is the way, the truth, and the life (see John 14:6).

So pivotal is Jesus in the divine plan that in 3:17–18 he becomes the point of decision and distinction between those who are saved and come to enjoy eternal life and those who are condemned. The Greek word for "judgment" is *krisis* (the origin of the English word "crisis"). It is one's attitude of belief toward Jesus ("the only Son of God") — for or against — that will determine where and how one stands before God.

The monologue ends in 3:19–21 with many images of light and darkness. Jesus is described as the light that has come into the world. Those who reject him love darkness rather than light, and so their deeds are evil. However, those who do what is true come to the light (Jesus), and so it can be clearly seen that their deeds have been done "in God."

The thrust of the Nicodemus episode in John 3:1–21 is to show how a religious seeker can move from darkness/night to light. Nicodemus came to Jesus by cover of darkness, and through his dialogue with Jesus and the monologue from the Johannine community has been shown the way to eternal life. In the larger Johannine narrative it appears that the instruction offered to Nicodemus had a positive effect. In John 7:50–52 Nicodemus defends Jesus in a meeting of Pharisees and asks that Jesus be given a fair hearing before condemning him. And in John 19:38 Nicodemus assists Joseph of Arimathea in seeing to the burial of Jesus.

3. The Samaritan Woman: From Puzzlement to Missionary Activity

> *"The Samaritan woman said to him, 'How is it that you, a Jew, ask a drink of me, a woman of Samaria?'"*
>
> — JOHN 4:9

Jesus' encounter with the Samaritan woman in John 4:1–42 is the first of several lengthy episodes in the first half of John's Gospel that gradually reveal the true identity of Jesus and show his impact on some unlikely persons. The narrative introduction in John 4:1–6 explains what Jesus was doing in Samaria. Apparently his success in attracting disciples had raised the hostility of the Pharisees, and so Jesus started back to Galilee. The idea that he "had to go through Samaria" is more a statement about his fulfilling the divine plan than about geography, since there were other routes he could have taken to avoid Samaria altogether. But the text suggests that it was God's will that his mission should extend into Samaria as part of historic Israel. In fact, the high point of the episode comes in 4:20–26 with Jesus' statement that in the near future proper worship of God will be conducted neither at Mount Gerizim (the site of the Samaritan sanctuary) nor at the Jerusalem temple (where Judeans and Galileans worshiped) but will be carried out "in spirit and truth." The encounter between Jesus and the Samaritan woman takes place at Sychar, a village in or near the biblical Shechem, at the site of Jacob's Well (see Genesis 33:18–19). It takes place about noon, when Jesus is tired from his travels.

Jesus initiates the encounter in John 4:7 with his request for a drink of water. The Samaritan woman is surprised by his request, either because she recognized him to be a Judean/Galilean (since there was a historic split with the Samaritans) and/or because there was dispute about the ritual purity of the vessels used by Samaritans. Jesus, however, raises the conversation to a new level in 4:10 when he begins to speak about "living water," that is, his own person and teaching that can lead to eternal life. The woman misunderstands and assumes that Jesus is talking about some hidden spring water. When Jesus corrects her and promises to give her the water that leads to eternal life, she eagerly asks that he give her such water, lest she have to keep coming back to the well for more water. When Jesus in 4:16–19 correctly tells her that she has had five husbands and is now living with a man who is not her husband, she concludes that he must be a prophet. Thus her perception of Jesus has grown from regarding him as just another Jew passing through Samaritan territory to his being a prophet.

In John 4:20–26, Jesus takes the conversation to an even higher level still when he declares that while salvation is from the Jews, the time is soon coming when the true worship of God will be "in spirit and truth," that is, not in an earthly sanctuary but wherever the Holy Spirit is. When the woman imagines that this will happen only in future messianic times, Jesus assures her that "I am he." With this phrase Jesus not only identifies himself as the Messiah but also suggests his divinity since "I AM" is a way in which God identifies himself in the Hebrew Scriptures (as in Exodus 3:14 and throughout Isaiah 40–55).

When in John 4:27–30 Jesus' disciples return and are surprised to see him conversing with a Samaritan woman, she leaves and goes back to the city and tells her fellow Samaritans that Jesus is not only a prophet but also may well be the Messiah. Thus she fulfills the role of a missionary on Jesus' behalf. She has moved from puzzlement at Jesus' presence and his request for water to the conviction that he is both the Prophet and the Messiah. She now not only more correctly identifies him but also attracts others to him.

Meanwhile in John 4:31–38 Jesus instructs his own inner circle of disciples about what he has to offer and how it can lead to eternal life. While before he used images of living water with the Samaritan woman, here he uses images of food and harvest. His "true" food is doing the will of his heavenly Father, and the harvest he envisions is the fullness of God's kingdom. Now he must recruit laborers to bring in that harvest. Those laborers, of course, are his disciples, those who will carry on the mission he has begun.

The Samaritan woman's missionary activity was successful to the point that in 4:39–42 we learn that many Samaritans believed her testimony, sought out Jesus for themselves, and came to believe in him and his teaching. Now their faith was based not only on the woman's testimony but also on their own personal contact with Jesus. And their experience led them to confess that Jesus is not only the Prophet and the Messiah but also (and especially) the Savior of the World (4:42).

The episode featuring Jesus and the Samaritan woman in John 4:1–42 traces a growth in recognizing the identity of Jesus from being just another Jew, to the Prophet and the Messiah, and to Savior of the World. It also shows how Jesus led the woman step-by-step to better understand him. And we see the woman move from her initial puzzlement at Jesus' request for a drink of water, through her greater insight into his character, to her missionary activity on his behalf, which issues in even more disciples and the even better perception of him as the Savior of the World.

4. The Man Born Blind: From Blindness to Sight

> *"The man called Jesus made mud, spread it on my eyes, and said to me, 'Go to Siloam and wash.' Then I went and washed and received my sight."*
>
> — JOHN 9:11

The sixth sign (see John 9:1–41) in the series of seven "signs" (or miracle stories) in John's Gospel concerns a man who was born blind. The episode takes place in Jerusalem. When the disciples ask whether it was the blind man or his parents who had sinned so as to cause his blindness, Jesus rejects that kind of thinking and indicates that his blindness will be an occasion for the revelation of God's glory from the one who is "the light of the world." The account of the healing in 9:6–7 smacks of magic, with Jesus' use of a mud paste made from his saliva smeared on the man's eyes and the man's washing in the Pool of Siloam. In any case, the procedure is successful and the blind man can now see.

The sign is the occasion for a series of five dialogues in which the formerly blind man comes to see clearly on a spiritual level who Jesus is, while the Jewish religious leaders who think they see clearly become increasingly blind spiritually.

In the first dialogue (9:8–12) his neighbors who had known him for many years debate whether this man who now can see was really the man who had always been blind. The man himself volunteers that he is one and the same, and describes in some detail how he has been healed by "the man called Jesus." When asked where Jesus is, he says noncommittally that he does not know.

In the second dialogue (9:13–17) the Pharisees are disturbed that the healing was performed on the Sabbath and so in their view Jesus broke the Sabbath law of rest from work. When they confront the man, he retells how Jesus healed him simply and straightforwardly. But the Pharisees contend that Jesus could not be from God since he does not observe the Sabbath properly, according to their standards. When they ask the man what he thinks, he now identifies Jesus as a prophet, a step up from "the man called Jesus," thus indicating his view that Jesus is from God and not from Satan.

The third dialogue (9:18–23) is between the "Jews" (the Jewish leaders hostile to Jesus) and the parents of the man born blind. When the Jews inquire about how their son came to see, the parents are deliberately evasive and say only that he was blind but now sees, and direct the Jews to ask the man himself. The reason for their evasion is supplied by the narrator, who claims that anyone who confessed Jesus to be the Messiah would be expelled from the synagogue (9:22; see also 12:42; 16:2).

In the fourth dialogue (9:24–34) the Jews summon the man and order him to accuse Jesus of being a sinner. The man, however, refuses to do so on the grounds that only someone from God could have healed his blindness. And he wonders why they are so persistent in refusing to see Jesus for who and what he is — someone from God. But the Jews remain convinced that they are the real disciples of Moses and are outraged when the man tries to teach them something about spiritual matters.

The fifth and final dialogue (9:35–41) is between Jesus and the man born blind. When Jesus encounters him again, he asks whether he believes in the Son of Man. In John's Gospel, of course, Son of Man is a very exalted title for Jesus. Though the man claims to believe in the Son of Man, he is not sure who the Son of Man is. When Jesus says that he is talking to the Son of Man, the man says, "Lord, I believe" and worships him.

Note the progression in spiritual sight that the man has passed through regarding Jesus from the time of his healing to his final encounter with Jesus: the man called Jesus (9:11), a prophet (9:17), the Messiah (9:22), a man from God (9:33), and the Son of Man (9:35) and Lord (9:38). As was the case with the Samaritan woman in John 4, this passage in John 9 traces the process of the man born blind's gradual enlightenment and growth in spiritual sight. Meanwhile those who thought they could see clearly in spiritual matters — the Pharisees/Jews — are revealed as spiritually blind to the meaning of the sign that has gone on right before their eyes. John 9 provides yet another case of unlikely persons who gradually come to greater clarity about Jesus as Jesus leads them on to faith in him as the revealer and revelation of God.

5. Martha and Mary: From Death to Life

"Then Jesus told them plainly, 'Lazarus is dead.'"

— John 11:14

While Lazarus seems to have been a friend and follower of Jesus before his death, Jesus' action in restoring him from death to life (John 11:1–44) is a pivotal moment in John's narrative about Jesus. It is the longest of the seven signs in the Fourth Gospel. It comes near the end of Jesus' public activity, and surely contributes to Jesus' arrest and death on the cross. It has some links with episodes in Luke's Gospel: the raising to life of the son of the widow of Nain (Luke 7:11–17), the hospitality shown by Mary and Martha (10:38–42), and the parable of the rich man and Lazarus (16:19–31). However, the narrative about Jesus' restoration of Lazarus to life after his death appears only in John's Gospel.

Even though the episode obviously concerns Lazarus as the central character next to Jesus, he never says a word. From the perspective of the theme of discipleship, what Martha and Mary have to say to Jesus and what Jesus has to say to them in response, and the development of their faith in Jesus, are most important. In John 11 we watch them move from faith in Jesus as a miracle worker and healer to recognition of him as "the resurrection and the life."

The center of the "sign" narrative in John 11:1–44 comes with Jesus' declaration in 11:25–26: "I am the resurrection and the life. Those who believe in me, even though they die, will live. And everyone who lives and believes in me will never die." The raising of Lazarus is not only a sign pointing to Jesus' own resurrection but also an anticipation of the resurrection of all those who become disciples of Jesus. It is a preview of the hope that can be found only in Jesus who is the way and the truth and the life. It also helps to explain the hostility of the Jewish leaders against Jesus and gives insight into the ultimate significance of Jesus' passion and death: victory over death, glory for the Son, and life for others.

The first section (11:1–6) introduces the characters and sets the scene for the miracle. Lazarus and his two sisters, named

Mary and Martha, live in Bethany, a village east of Jerusalem. When Lazarus falls ill, the sisters send a messenger to Jesus in the hope that he will come and heal their brother. They describe Lazarus as someone whom Jesus loved, thus leading some scholars to speculate that Lazarus may be the mysterious Beloved Disciple of the Fourth Gospel. Indeed Jesus is said to love all three of these characters. But instead of coming immediately, Jesus delays for a few days, on the grounds that "this is for God's glory."

The second section (11:7–16) establishes in two dialogues between Jesus and his disciples Jesus' resolve to go to Jerusalem and the fact that Lazarus was already dead. When the disciples remind Jesus of the danger he might face in Jerusalem, he insists that he must act while it is still light, that is, during his public ministry that will soon come to a close and be replaced by the darkness of the passion. Then when he announces that Lazarus "has fallen asleep," the disciples misunderstand him, and so Jesus comes straight out and says quite brutally, "Lazarus is dead."

The central section (11:17–27) sets the scene at Bethany and presents a dialogue between Jesus and Martha. Lazarus was already dead and buried. Many of "the Jews" had come to console the two sisters. When Martha hears that Jesus was finally coming, she goes out to meet him. When she suggests that perhaps Jesus could have healed Lazarus if he had come earlier, he replies that Lazarus "will rise again." Martha takes this to mean in the resurrection of the dead at the end of human history. Jesus, however, declares himself to be "the resurrection and the life" right here and now, thus making himself the point of reference for belief in eternal life. Even Martha's confession of Jesus as the Messiah and Son of God, while accurate, does not go far enough. She must come to see that he is the resurrection and the life.

The fourth section (11:28–37) features a conversation between Jesus and Mary, and highlights Jesus' emotional attachment to Lazarus and his sisters. Both Mary and the Jews provide more veiled criticisms of Jesus by again suggesting that if he had been there he might have healed Lazarus. Mary and the Jews still regard Jesus as a healer and miracle worker. They too do not go far enough in identifying Jesus. They too must come to see that he is the resurrection and the life.

The final section (11:38–44) describes the removal of the stone from the mouth of Lazarus' tomb, Jesus' command for him to come out of the tomb, and his emergence as alive again. It also specifies the purpose of restoring Lazarus to life. It is intended as a manifestation of the glory of God, with the hope of bringing others to believe that God is the one who has sent Jesus. That is, the action should serve to make more disciples of Jesus. And according to John 11:45 it did. However, the irony is that this spectacular display of life-giving power on Jesus' part, according to John, led the Jewish leaders to plot Jesus' death (11:47–53) and even to devise a plot to kill Lazarus (12:9–11).

What happened to Lazarus was not yet the same as the resurrection of Jesus. It can be assumed that Lazarus after his recovery at some point in life would die again. Thus he underwent something like what we might call a resuscitation, though having been dead for a very long period of time. But Jesus' restoration of him to life is an anticipation of his own full-scale resurrection to eternal glory. If the restoration of Lazarus meant an increase among Jesus' disciples, how much more could, should, and would the resurrection of Jesus mean! And if indeed Lazarus was the Beloved Disciple, this episode would explain why in what follows in the rest of John's Gospel the Beloved Disciple becomes such a major figure and example of the ideal of Johannine discipleship.

6. Easter Witnesses: From Confusion to Confession of Faith

> *"They have taken the Lord out of the tomb, and we do not know where they have laid him."*
>
> — JOHN 20:2

All four Gospels agree that Mary Magdalene witnessed the death of Jesus on Good Friday, saw where he was buried, went to his tomb on Easter Sunday morning, and found it empty. The questions facing her and other disciples of Jesus were: How did his tomb get empty? What happened to Jesus' corpse? What did its disappearance mean?

John 20 deals with that question by pointing to the resurrection of Jesus as the proper explanation, and charts the development of faith in it on the part of his first followers. There are four major episodes: Peter and the "other" disciple at the tomb (20:1–10), Jesus' appearance to Mary Magdalene (20:11–18), his appearance to most of the inner circle of disciples (20:19–23), and his appearance to them and to Thomas (20:24–29). In these episodes the disciples of Jesus move from doubt to faith and from confusion to clarity.

According to John 20:1–10, Mary Magdalene came to the tomb on Easter Sunday and found it empty. In her confusion she ran to Peter and the "other" disciple (who is presumably the Beloved Disciple), who in turn engage in a kind of foot race back to the tomb. Peter, too, finds it empty, thus confirming Mary's original interpretation that Jesus' body had been "taken." However, when the Beloved Disciple enters the tomb and finds it remarkably neat, we are told that "he saw and believed." He may well have deduced from the neat disposition of the burial cloths that Jesus' corpse had not been taken by humans but by God.

In John 20:11–18 Mary Magdalene is the first recipient of an appearance of the risen Jesus (see also Matthew 28:9–10). She is standing outside Jesus' tomb, and is weeping because she is convinced that Jesus' body has been stolen. When she encounters a mysterious stranger, she fails to recognize that he is Jesus and imagines that he is the gardener. Only when Jesus calls her by her name, "Mary," does she recognize him to be the risen Jesus. Jesus' command to her, "Do not hold on to me" in 20:17 has fascinated, puzzled, and eluded interpreters for many centuries. However, the main point is that Mary has experienced her friend Jesus whom she saw die as fully alive again, that is, as raised from the dead. And so when she goes and tells the other disciples "I have seen the Lord" in 20:18, she fulfills her vocation to be the apostle to the apostles.

The first appearance of the risen Jesus to the inner circle of his disciples (20:19–23) takes place on Easter Sunday afternoon. His mysterious entry through locked doors (stressing the spiritual side of his resurrected existence) is balanced by his showing them the wounds on his body (thus stressing the material side). He wishes them "Peace" twice, and empowers them with the gift of the Holy Spirit to carry on the work he himself received from his heavenly Father: "As the Father has sent me, so I send you" (20:21). He also grants them power over sin (see Matthew 16:19; 18:18).

One of the disciples, Thomas, was absent at the first of Jesus' appearances to the inner circle of disciples. And so, according to John 20:24–25, he is skeptical about their talk of an appearance of the risen Jesus. He claims that he will believe only if he can touch the body of Jesus and feel the wounds in his body. On the following Sunday, according to John 20:26–29, Thomas finds himself with the other disciples. The risen Jesus suddenly appears among them. Again Jesus wishes them all "Peace," and invites (and challenges) Thomas to touch the places of the wounds on his body. Thomas, however, is immediately and completely convinced that Jesus has been truly raised from the dead, and so he utters the highest confession of faith in Jesus in the Fourth Gospel, "My Lord and my God!" (20:28). This confession echoes that description of Jesus that opened the Gospel, "In the beginning was the Word, and the Word was with God, and the Word was God" (1:1).

The disciples have finally come to see Jesus for who and what he truly is ("My Lord and my God"), when they experience him as having been raised from the dead. Jesus, however, declares that there is an even higher form of faith in him that is displayed by those who have not been privileged to see the risen Jesus and yet still believe in him, "Blessed are those who have not seen and yet have come to believe" (20:29). This definition fits all those who read John's Gospel and who "come to believe that Jesus is the Messiah and the Son of God, and that through believing have life in his name" (20:31).

Bringing the Texts Together

The stories about discipleship in John's Gospel are different from those in the other Gospels. They are obviously longer and more leisurely in the telling. In them Jesus leads persons from an at-best mild curiosity about him and his mission to a more mature appreciation of him and his mission.

In John 1:43–51 Nathanael moves from initial scorn of Jesus' origins in Nazareth, through a confession of him as the Messiah and Son of God, to envisioning him as the glorious Son of Man. In 3:1–21 Nicodemus, a Pharisee and Jewish leader, seeks out Jesus by night and learns about the greatness of Jesus and how he too can become a child of the light.

The Samaritan woman in John 4:1–42 moves from bafflement over why a Jewish teacher would ask her for a drink of water at Jacob's Well to identifying him as the Prophet and the Messiah, and undertaking missionary activity on his behalf as the Savior of the world. Likewise, the man born blind in John 9:1–41 moves from his physical blindness to recognizing Jesus as the Son of Man and Lord.

The two sisters of Lazarus, Martha and Mary, in John 11:1–44 move from faith in Jesus as a powerful healer to his identity as the resurrection and the life. So too in John 20:1–31 various followers of Jesus — the Beloved Disciple, Mary Magdalene, the inner circle of disciples, and Thomas — come to see with increasing clarity and confidence that God has indeed raised Jesus from the dead to new life, and that he is worthy of the titles "my Lord and my God."

THINK, PRAY, AND ACT

THINK

1. How did you come to follow Jesus? Was it quick (as in the Synoptics) or gradual (as in John)?
2. Has your appreciation of God and Jesus changed over the years? If so, how?
3. What understandings of God (and/or Jesus) that you once held might now seem inappropriate or not helpful?

PRAY

Choose three of the many titles applied to Jesus in John's Gospel, and repeat them slowly and prayerfully for a few minutes.

Ask God for the grace to make progress in your own appreciation of Jesus and how you might better reflect his values and attitudes in your life.

ACT

Volunteer to become part of a discussion/prayer group at your church during Advent or Lent, and suggest the theme of "Following Jesus."

3

Paul
as a Disciple of Jesus

Next to Jesus, Paul is the most prominent figure in the New Testament. Of its twenty-seven books, thirteen letters are attributed to Paul, and half of Acts is about Paul. Paul moves the story of following Jesus forward after Jesus' resurrection and into the formation and development of the early church. By focusing on Paul as a disciple of Jesus, we can grasp the call to discipleship as it occurs in the light of Easter, and see how he carried out his special vocation to bring the gospel to those who had not yet heard it.

1. Paul's Call

> *"But when God, who had set me apart before I was born and called me through his grace, was pleased to reveal his Son to me, so that I might proclaim him among the Gentiles, I did not confer with any human being."*
>
> — Galatians 1:15–16

In his letter to the Galatians, Paul describes his own call to the life of discipleship in a remarkably concise manner. The Galatians lived in what is now central Turkey (ancient Asia Minor). They were descendants of Celtic mercenaries who had settled in the area centuries before, and had become Christians through the ministry of Paul the apostle when some physical ailment forced him to spend time with them (see Galatians 4:12–14). After Paul had completed his work among them and had founded the Christian community there, Paul in accord with his practice then moved on to other areas in order to found new churches (see Romans 15:20–21).

In Paul's absence there arrived in Galatia a group of Jewish-Christian missionaries from Jerusalem who tried to convince the Galatian Christians that they had to convert to Judaism, undergo circumcision, and observe the Sabbath and food laws in order to become true and authentic Christians. The Galatian Christians were Gentiles (not Jews) and Paul had told them nothing of the sort. The rival missionaries began to tear down Paul's reputation as an apostle and to suggest that Paul was not an authentic and reliable Christian teacher.

Word got back to Paul about the situation in Galatia. And Paul wrote a fiery letter in the mid-50s of the first century A.D. in defense of his preaching of the gospel. He saw that what was at stake was the truth of his gospel and ultimately the saving significance of Jesus' death and resurrection (the core of his gospel). Paul was fully convinced that since the Gentile Christians at Galatia had received the Holy Spirit, there was no need for them to convert to Judaism (3:1–5). In fact, to do so would call into question the value or efficacy of Jesus' death and resurrection in the divine plan and their own reception of the Holy Spirit.

Paul's letter to the Galatians is by far his most emotional writing. He dispenses with the good wishes conveyed in the conventional thanksgiving section, and gets right into his argument by stating his astonishment (1:6) that the Galatian Christians were paying attention to the proposals of the Jewish Christian missionaries from Jerusalem. Later in the letter (3:1), he addresses them in very strong terms, "You foolish Galatians! Who has bewitched you?"

Early in the letter (1:14) Paul appeals to his own credentials as a Jew, "I advanced in Judaism beyond many among my people of the same age, for I was far more zealous for the traditions of my ancestors." Then in Galatians 3:6–29 Paul constructs an elaborate and complicated argument based on a variety of Old Testament passages to prove that people of faith — regardless of their ethnicity — are the real children of Abraham. What far outweighed Paul's ethnic-religious background and his vast Jewish learning was his experience of the risen Jesus on the road to Damascus.

The story of what is commonly known as Paul's "conversion" is related in great detail three times in the Acts of the Apostles (9:1–19; 22:3–21; and 26:12–18). There Paul tells how he, once the persecutor of the Christian movement, experienced the risen Jesus in some kind of profound religious experience and received a special commission or vocation to become an apostle to non-Jews and to bring to them the good news (the gospel) about the saving significance of Jesus' death and resurrection.

Paul's own account of his experience in Galatians 1:15–16 is a model of conciseness. Of course, he is not writing an autobiography. Rather, he is making an argument. And essential to Paul's argument is his conviction that he received directly his call or commission to bring the gospel to non-Jews in the course of his experience of the risen Jesus. In describing himself, he uses terms found in the Old Testament with reference to the call of the prophet Jeremiah, "But when God, who had set me apart before I was born and called me through his grace" (Galatians 1:15; see Jeremiah 1:5).

Biblical scholars have long debated whether we should describe what happened to Paul on the road to Damascus as a "conversion" or a "call." If we do opt for "conversion," it is important to note that in Paul's time it would have been viewed as a conversion from one kind of Judaism (Pharisaic) to another kind of Judaism (Christian), not from one religion (Judaism) to another (Christianity). Moreover, what seems central in Paul's own account and present in all the accounts in Acts (and repeatedly alluded to throughout Paul's own letters) is the special call to serve as a missionary to non-Jews, "[God] was pleased to reveal his Son to me, so that I might proclaim him among the Gentiles." It is both a conversion and a call, or a conversion with a special calling attached.

Paul goes on to insist that he received his call and commission directly from the risen Christ. In the salutation of the letter (1:1) he introduces himself as "an apostle — sent neither by human commission nor from human authorities, but through Jesus Christ and God the Father, who raised him from the dead." After denying in 1:16 that he conferred with any human being about all this, he goes on to say that only after three years did he confer with Cephas/Peter and James in Jerusalem, and that they confirmed him in his mission and glorified God because of him.

Paul was a disciple of the risen Jesus. He makes no claim to have known the earthly Jesus. In fact, he repeatedly refers to the fact that he had persecuted the movement begun by Jesus.

Yet something so powerful and remarkable happened to Paul on the road to Damascus that everything changed. What he once regarded as a dangerous aberration and a threat to Judaism, he came to see as the goal toward which everything in the heritage of his people Israel had been pointing. Now his whole existence was wrapped up in the Christ-event. Nothing better summarizes Paul's new existence than his own words in his letter to the Philippians, "I want to know Christ and the power of his resurrection and the sharing of his sufferings by becoming like him in his death, if somehow I may attain the resurrection from the dead" (3:10–11).

2. Paul as a Minister of the Word

> *"We also constantly give thanks to God for this, that when you received the word of God that you heard from us, you accepted it not as a human word but as what it really is, God's word, which is also at work in you believers."*
>
> — 1 THESSALONIANS 2:13

Like Jesus and his first followers in Palestine, Paul went about the cities and towns of the Greco-Roman world, trying to convince any people who might listen that God was doing something new and important in the world. The focus of Paul's preaching was the death and resurrection of Jesus of Nazareth. He was especially concerned to show the possibilities for right relationship with God that Jesus opened up in the present and promised for the future as preparation for the full coming of God's kingdom. This was the "good news," or gospel, that Paul never tired of preaching.

As Paul went about the cities of modern Turkey (ancient Asia Minor) and Greece, he traveled largely on foot, and supported himself along the way as a leather worker or tent maker while often relying on the kindness of strangers for lodging and food. One of the cities on his route was Thessalonica in northern Greece. There according to Acts 17:1–9 Paul's preaching about Jesus in the local synagogue caused an uproar and even got him arrested briefly. He and his companions were accused of "turning the world upside down." Eventually Paul founded a Christian community in Thessalonica, and once he judged it to be on relatively firm foundations he moved on to another community to start still another church. This is how Paul conceived his apostolic task of preaching the gospel of Jesus Christ: proclaiming the gospel where it had not yet been heard.

Paul's First Letter to the Thessalonians is generally regarded as the earliest extant document in the New Testament. Paul's letters were one way in which he kept in contact with the Christians in the churches he had founded. Through his team of coworkers he received reports on the progress the new Christians were making and the problems they were facing. In some cases the new Christians wrote directly to Paul (see 1 Corinthians 7:1). His letters were mainly responses to their concerns. We should not imagine Paul as a scholarly professor writing theological treatises in his office. No. Paul was a founder of churches and a pastoral theologian. He was always trying to shed the light of the gospel on the real issues that his people were confronting in their efforts at putting their newfound Christianity into practice.

Paul's coworker Timothy had given Paul a good first-hand report about the Thessalonian Christians, and Paul planned to visit them personally again. In the meantime he wrote a letter to encourage them in their pursuit of holiness, to be careful about personal relationships within the community, and to help them deal with the fact that some members had died and this had led to anxieties about their possible non-participation in the second coming of Christ and the full coming of God's kingdom.

In responding to these issues, Paul first praised the Thessalonians' faith and good example, and tried to encourage them about their good progress. Then he reminded them of his own ministry in Thessalonica and the personal relationship he had built up with them. However, Paul was especially concerned to remind them that in his ministry Paul was only an instrument of God's word and he rejoiced that they accepted his preaching not as his own word but rather as the word of God active among them.

And so Paul writes, "We also constantly give thanks to God for this, that when you received the word of God that you heard from us, you accepted it not as a human word but as what it really is, God's word, which is also at work among you believers" (2:13). Thus he invokes the biblical concept of the word of God as something dynamic and effective in its own right, as "living and active, sharper than any two-edged sword" (Hebrews 4:12). Paul's discipleship took the form of the ministry of the word, and the word he preached concerned the saving effects of Jesus' death and resurrection.

Yet Paul's discipleship did not come without opposition. In leading up to his beautiful conclusion in 2:13, Paul recalls in 2:1–2 the sufferings he underwent at Philippi (see Acts 16:16–40) and the opposition he faced at Thessalonica (see Acts 17:1–9). In 2:3–6 he refutes charges made against him that he was a charlatan and a flatterer, and not an authentic apostle "approved by God to be entrusted with the message of the gospel." One proof of his authenticity was the fact that he refused to make use of the "demands" customarily offered an apostle of Christ (2:7). That is, Paul did not avail himself of the material support that was due him as an apostle. Instead, he insisted on supporting himself by working with his hands, precisely to avoid the charge of seeking his own comfort and pleasure.

What Paul was most eager to do was to share the gospel of God (the saving effects of Jesus' death and resurrection) and in the process to share his own self. In 2:7 he compares himself to a nurse "tenderly caring for her own children." If a hired nurse might be expected to care properly for her employer's children, how much more carefully would she care for her own children! In 2:10 Paul characterizes his own conduct with the Thessalonians as "pure, upright, and blameless." In 2:11–12 he also compares himself to a loving father "urging and encouraging you and pleading that you live a life worthy of God."

Paul's call to discipleship took the form of the ministry of proclaiming the word of God (the gospel about the crucified and risen Jesus) to those who had not heard it before. He was convinced that this call came directly from the risen Jesus. And he was so consumed by it and so committed to this ministry that everything else took a distant second place. And so he tried to cultivate a way of life that was in perfect harmony with carrying out his call.

3. God's Power Made Perfect in Weakness

> *"Three times I appealed to the Lord about this, that it would leave me, but he said to me, 'My grace is sufficient for you, for power is made perfect in weakness.' So I will boast all the more gladly of my weaknesses, so that the power of Christ may dwell in me."*
>
> — 2 CORINTHIANS 12:8–9

Despite his divine calling, Paul had human opponents, some of them fellow Christians. Their complaints were both personal and theological. According to Paul's own testimony in 2 Corinthians 10:10, they were saying that "his letters are weighty and strong, but his bodily presence is weak and his speech contemptible." While admitting Paul's ability as a letter writer, some apparently dismissed Paul because of his unimpressive physical presence. This was especially important in a culture in which some people made correlations between a person's physical presence and his character and ability (the science of physiognomy). The only ancient description of Paul's physical bearing comes from the second-century *Acts of Paul and Thecla*: "A man small of stature, with a bald head and crooked legs, a good state of body, with eyebrows meeting and nose somewhat hooked, full of friendliness." Of course, there is no guarantee that this description was entirely accurate or came from anyone who knew Paul personally.

The second charge in 10:10 was that Paul's speech was "contemptible." Paul (and all the characters in the New Testament) lived and worked in a largely oral culture in which skill in public speaking was often the criterion by which persons were judged. The charge of "contemptible" speech may refer simply to Paul having a weak voice or even some speech impediment. Or it could refer to a perceived lack of rhetorical polish in Paul's speeches. Paul's letters indicate that Paul had been exposed to some level of the rhetorical education that was available to males as they grew to maturity. The curriculum featured the various techniques and devices developed as part of the art of persuasion in the schools of the time in the Greco-Roman world. It also included reading speeches by famous orators of the past and imitating their language and techniques.

Another source of opposition to Paul centered around the theological legitimacy of his Law-free gospel for Gentiles. An essential part of Paul's call was to preach the saving significance of Jesus' death and resurrection to non-Jews. He had become convinced on the basis of his own experience that his Gentile converts did not have to convert to Judaism and to observe the distinctive identity markers of Jews in the Greco-Roman world: circumcision, Sabbath observance, and laws about food and ritual purity. More importantly, he had come to see that these Gentile Christians had received the Holy Spirit and were living in right relationship with God and other persons by reason of their faith in Christ (justification), and that to force them to become Jews would be to deny the efficacy of Christ's death and resurrection in bringing about this blessed state.

However, some of Paul's fellow Jewish Christians did not see things the way he did. Since they still conceived of their new Christian movement as a sect within Judaism, they assumed that those non-Jews who had become part of it would take the next obvious step and become full-fledged Jews. But Paul resisted their reasoning when it came to persons whom he had brought to Christian faith. So in several of Paul's letters (Galatians, Philippians, 2 Corinthians, and Romans) there is evidence of vigorous opposition to Paul from other Jewish-Christian missionaries. These people were apparently following Paul around and contradicting his teaching that Gentiles did not have to become Jews in order to be fully authentic Christians.

In his letters to the Galatians and Philippians, Paul takes an aggressive and sometimes even nasty stance toward his detractors. He goes so far as to accuse them of having "bewitched" the Galatians (3:1) and in Philippians 3:2 of being "dogs" and of "mutilating the flesh" with their insistence on circumcision. However, in 2 Corinthians, especially in chapters 10–13, he is more thoughtful, subtle, and effective. Rather than defending himself by denying his opponents' charges, Paul in 2 Corinthians 11 calls himself a "fool" and proceeds to "boast of things that show my weakness" (11:30). That means most dramatically providing a list of what he had suffered in carrying out his mission as an apostle: his imprisonments and physical abuse, his dangerous travels, and his many other deprivations for the sake of his mission. Passing over briefly his mystical experiences in 12:1–4, Paul dismisses such talk as foolishness and speaks of his somewhat mysterious "thorn in the flesh" in 12:7. Scholarly speculations about its precise nature range from epilepsy to a speech impediment, and practically everything in between. Instead of spending time in identifying the "thorn," Paul prefers to interpret it as something allowed by God to keep him "from being too elated," that is, from becoming too proud and boastful. He does, however, describe his repeated prayers that the Lord might relieve him of this burden as being of no avail. But he does receive resolution when the Lord tells him, "My grace is sufficient for you, for power is made perfect in weakness" (12:8).

Paul's great insight was that his personal limitations and weaknesses could allow the power and glory of God to shine forth ever more brightly. He no longer had to worry about concealing his shortcomings, because it is through them that Christ was most at work. Paul summarizes his insight and his situation in 12:10: "Therefore I am content with weaknesses, insults, hardships, persecutions and calamities for the sake of Christ, for when I am weak, then I am strong." That is perfect freedom. That is perfect application of Jesus' own teaching about discipleship in Mark 8:35: "Those who lose their life for my sake and for the sake of the gospel will save it." This is what Paul himself meant in 1 Corinthians 1–4 when he wrote about the cross of Christ being the wisdom of God: "For God's foolishness is wiser than human wisdom, and God's weakness is stronger than human strength" (1:25).

4. Paul's Priestly Service

> *"Nevertheless on some points I have written to you rather boldly by way of reminder, because of the grace given me by God to be a minister of Christ Jesus to the Gentiles in the priestly service of the gospel of God, so that the offering of the Gentiles may be acceptable, sanctified by the Holy Spirit."*
>
> — Romans 15:15–16

Paul's letter to the Romans is justly famous as the great synthesis of the apostle's theology. In it he first establishes in chapters 1–4 that both Gentiles and Jews had need for the revelation of God's righteousness (or covenant fidelity) in Jesus, and that the way by which both groups might share in the new relationship with God was through faith after the example of Abraham. Then in chapters 5–8 he reflects on how Jesus' death and resurrection has freed us from the power of Sin, Death, and the Law, and made it possible for us all to live as children of God under the guidance of the Holy Spirit. Next in chapters 9–11 he meditates on the working out of God's plan for the history of salvation, with historic Israel represented now by Paul and other Jewish Christians as the root of the olive tree, Gentile Christians as branches broken off from a wild olive tree and grafted onto the cultivated olive tree, and other Jews eventually returning to the olive tree ("And so all Israel will be saved," 11:25). Then from chapter 12 onward he gives ethical advice on various topics, and deals with a conflict between two groups of Christians at Rome. The "end" material in chapters 15–16 tends to be neglected in favor of the more obviously theologically important parts of the letter.

However, it is in Romans 15–16 that we learn much about how Paul the apostle understood and carried out his call to discipleship. To describe this as "strategy" is perhaps to debase or trivialize it. It is better regarded as the concrete realization of Paul's vocation to be the apostle to the Gentiles. In Romans 15:16 he describes it as "the priestly service of the gospel of God." Of course, by Jewish standards Paul could never have been a priest, since he was from the tribe of Benjamin (see Philippians 3:5), not of the tribe of Levi (from which legitimate Jewish priests came). And to regard Paul as a Christian ministerial priest would be premature from a historical perspective. Rather, Paul here is using metaphorical language to describe his ministry as the apostle to the Gentiles.

In the ancient world the most obvious activity associated with priesthoods, whether Jewish or pagan, was offering sacrifices to God. Those sacrifices were understood fundamentally as gifts to God. They might serve to strengthen the bonds between God and those making the offering, to give thanks for the reception of divine favors, or to atone for sins committed consciously or unconsciously. In Romans 15:15–16 Paul conceives his work in bringing Gentiles to right relationship with the God of Israel and the Lord Jesus Christ in terms of sacrifices and priesthood. He describes his Gentile mission as a sacrifice or gift to God, his own work as "priestly service," and the Holy Spirit as the one who has sanctified the offering.

When introducing this metaphor, Paul invokes his divine call to serve as the apostle to the Gentiles ("because of the grace given me by God") and admits that he has written to the Romans "rather boldly." Unlike his letters to other communities, Romans was addressed to a community that Paul had not founded. In fact, Paul had never been to Rome prior to his writing his letter around A.D. 56 or 57. One of his reasons for writing was to request the hospitality of the Roman Christians as he traveled westward to begin a new mission in Spain. Writing such a long letter was surely an act of boldness on Paul's part. A short note might have done just as well to secure lodging. Moreover, Paul went so far in his boldness as to offer advice on conflicts within the Roman community, especially relationships there between Jewish Christians and Gentile Christians. He probably also wanted to take the occasion to introduce himself to the Roman Christians (who surely had heard about him) and to defend his Law-free gospel for Gentile Christians. Before coming to Rome, Paul planned to bring the proceeds of the collection to the Christians at Jerusalem. He very likely anticipated having to explain himself there too, and so the letter to the Romans was also a kind of rehearsal for his anticipated meeting with the church leaders there.

The principle underlying Paul's apostolic activity was to keep on founding new Christian communities, and so spread the gospel all over the Mediterranean world. In his geographical perspective Spain qualified as "the ends of the earth." In Romans 15:20 Paul states, "Thus I make it my ambition to proclaim the good news not where Christ has already been named, so that I do not build on someone else's foundation." That explains why Paul was so eager to travel and why he founded so many new churches. He was being obedient to the call to discipleship that he had received from the risen Christ on the road to Damascus.

It would be wrong to imagine that Paul carried out his mission all alone. On the contrary, Paul clearly worked in collaboration with a team or network of fellow Christians beyond his closest associates, Timothy and Titus. His greetings from Corinth (where he wrote) to Christians at Rome in Romans 16:1–16 illustrates this point concretely. First he commends Phoebe the deacon and asks that she be warmly received at Rome. She may well have been carrying Paul's letter to Rome. Then he mentions Prisca (known as Priscilla in Acts) and Aquila, a married couple, as his coworkers, along with several other men and women. He describes Andronicus and Junia (probably another married couple) as "prominent among the apostles." The list is a reminder that the early church consisted of a variety of persons, male and female, Jews and Gentiles, slaves and free. What brought these people together was the good news that Paul the disciple of the risen Jesus proclaimed about Jesus and the saving effects of his life, death, and resurrection.

5. All Are One in Christ Jesus

> *"Perhaps this is the reason he was separated from you for a while, so that you might have him back forever, no longer as a slave but more than a slave, a beloved brother — especially to me but how much more to you, both in the flesh and in the Lord."*
>
> — PHILEMON 15–16

Paul's letter to Philemon is the shortest of his epistles in the Christian canon of Scripture. It is only one chapter, and not easy to understand on first reading. So it tends to be neglected. However, paying attention to it can help us to see Paul the apostle in action, dealing with the concrete realities of life in the Mediterranean world in the first century, and highlighting the importance of being a disciple of Jesus.

One of those realities was slavery. It has been estimated that a third of the persons living in the Roman Empire had been slaves at some point in their lives. One of those persons was a slave named Onesimus, who belonged to a Christian named Philemon. Paul was the one who had brought Philemon to Christian faith. It seems that Onesimus the slave of Philemon had run away from his household, a very serious crime in the Roman Empire. The text of the letter ("if he has wronged you in any way, or owes you anything," v. 18) suggests that he may have been guilty of some financial irregularity.

Meanwhile, when Paul was imprisoned, perhaps under a kind of house arrest in Ephesus, Onesimus sought him out as a potential mediator with his master, and under Paul's direction he became a Christian too. Through his letter to Philemon, Paul wanted to arrange to have Philemon take Onesimus back into his household without any penalty. In fact, Onesimus (his name means "useful"), who was now useless to Philemon, had become useful to Paul, and Paul was even tempted to keep him on as his assistant of some sort. However, Paul finally decided to inform Philemon about what had happened to Onesimus, thus giving him the option to receive the runaway back into his household.

It appears that Philemon's household was the place where the early Christians in the area (perhaps at Colossae) gathered for their regular meetings and celebrations of the Eucharist. It also is very likely that Paul's letter to Philemon was read publicly at one of the gatherings held in Philemon's household. The main point of Paul's letter was his request that Philemon should take Onesimus back not only without a penalty but even and especially no longer as a slave but rather as "a beloved brother" (v. 16). Whether Paul expected Philemon to give Onesimus his freedom is not clear. However, near the end, Paul does express confidence that Philemon "will do even more than I say" (21). That might mean freeing Onesimus. What is clear is that Paul wants his convert Philemon to regard his slave and now fellow Christian Onesimus as his equal at least in the sight of God and Christ and of his fellow Christians.

In other words, for Paul, Christian identity transcends or trumps social distinctions. In his letter to the Galatians (3:28), he quoted what seems to have been part of an early Christian baptismal slogan, "There is no longer Jew or Greek, there is no longer slave or free, there is no longer male and female; for all of you are one in Christ Jesus." It is through faith and baptism that all kinds of persons can and do become disciples of Jesus Christ. What is most important about them is no longer their ethnic identity, social status, or gender. While these identity markers do not disappear, they are at least relativized in comparison with the now greater identity marker of being "in Christ."

Paul's suggestion about taking Onesimus back as a "beloved brother" would have been very difficult for Philemon. He lived in a society in which such distinctions were very important, and in which much of economy was based on slave labor. To persuade him to look upon his runaway slave Onesimus as now a beloved brother, Paul used many of the tools of rhetoric. He praised Philemon's love and faith; he ostensibly left the decision up to him while informing the entire community gathered in his house about the matter; he reminded him how much he owed Paul for bringing him to Christian faith; and he promised to visit him personally as soon as possible. That is how important that Paul felt about the primacy of Christian identity in a person's life. He was convinced that all kinds of persons can and should become disciples of Christ, because he envisioned a world in which all might be one in Christ.

6. Paul's Example of Self-Sacrificing Love

"Be imitators of me, as I am of Christ."

— 1 Corinthians 11:1

There is a longstanding discussion among Pauline specialists as to which of his letters is the most important for students to read first and so get a sense of what Paul was really about. Some say Romans, since it at least approaches being a synthesis of Paul's great theological insights into what God has done in Jesus. The fact that many great Christian theologians throughout the centuries have written learned commentaries on Romans reinforces the perception of its centrality. However, other scholars, those perhaps especially interested in the development of the Christian church in the context of the Greco-Roman world, argue for 1 Corinthians. That letter, they say, allows us to see firsthand the kind of difficulties that early Christians fell into as they tried to navigate their lives in accord with their newfound Christian faith. It also has the advantage of watching Paul respond to their problems and provide guidance to them. Here I will focus on 1 Corinthians.

Paul is best described, I believe, as a pastoral theologian. He was not a professor writing books in the quiet of his office, with occasional trips to the library. He was basically a founder of churches, and his letters were occasional compositions designed primarily to encourage and direct those whom he had brought to Christian faith. Once Paul had founded a church and saw that it was on track, he moved on to other places in order to found other churches. His guiding principle was, as we have seen, to proclaim the good news wherever Christ had not "already been named" (Romans 15:20). His letters were thus ways of staying in touch with those churches that he had founded and of giving his advice on the pastoral problems that they were encountering.

In most cases Paul had few precedents for his pastoral advice. What he generally was doing was looking at a pastoral problem or difficulty, and offering advice in the light of his convictions about the implications of Jesus' life, death, and resurrection. So profound was Paul's identification with Christ that he was convinced that he had "the mind of Christ" (1 Corinthians 2:16), and that he was saying and doing what Jesus would have said and did if he had been in Paul's position. Or at least, what Paul was saying was in his view coherent and consistent with what was most important about Jesus, as this was expressed in early Christian confessions of faith, such as "Christ died for our sins in accordance with the scriptures" (1 Corinthians 15:3).

In 1 Corinthians Paul deals with a wide variety of difficulties and problems that had arisen in the church at Corinth after he had moved on to found other churches. They included factions within the community, sexual immorality, lawsuits between Christians, confusion about marriage and celibacy, eating food associated with pagan cults, disorder in the Christian assembly and at celebrations of the Lord's Supper, the relative importance of spiritual gifts, and the resurrection of Christ.

Near the end of Paul's advice about dealing with factions within the community at Corinth, Paul appeals to the Christians there to "be imitators of me" (4:16). And also near the end of his attempt at adjudicating the dispute about eating food associated with pagan cults, Paul in 11:1 writes, "Be imitators of me, as I am of Christ."

What does this claim mean? What did it mean for Paul to imitate Christ? It is unlikely that Paul ever met the earthly Jesus in person. And so the imitation to which he refers could not mean imitating Jesus' clothing, lifestyle, mannerisms, or speech. It must have been something more basic. Was it Jesus' teaching? However, Paul seldom quotes sayings of Jesus or uses Jesus' teachings in the course of an argument. Some rare exceptions include Jesus' teaching on marriage and divorce in 1 Corinthians 7:10–11 and his words at the Last Supper in 1 Corinthians 11:23–26. But Paul does not seem to have used whatever sayings of Jesus he knew as the basis for his imitation of him.

There must have been something even more profound about Jesus than his external mannerisms or even his teachings that Paul viewed as especially worthy of imitation. The most likely explanation seems to have been Jesus' self-sacrificing love, his willingness to be a "man for others," to that point of giving up his own life so that others might enjoy along with him the new and intimate relationship with God that comes with being children of God (Romans 8:16–17).

Just as Jesus set aside his own self for the sake of others in his passion and death, so Paul declares himself willing to do likewise on behalf of others. And so he urges those who had become disciples through him to do the same. That fits with his appeal for imitation in 1 Corinthians 4:16. It comes at the end of Paul's advice about dealing with factions. Some people at Corinth were apparently appealing to the apostle who had brought them to faith (Cephas, Apollos, or Paul). Paul, however, regarded such disputes as foolish, because what really counts is baptism into Jesus' death and resurrection and the new status as God's children that it made possible. The important figure is Christ, not apostles like Paul. And so Paul declares himself to be only an instrument in bringing the gospel to the Corinthians. Just as he denigrates his own personal importance, so should the participants in the dispute at Corinth set aside their alleged spiritual importance, and find their unity in their common baptism in Christ Jesus.

Likewise with 1 Corinthians 11:1, Paul's call to be imitators of him "as he is of Christ" comes at the end of a long and complicated treatment (in 1 Corinthians 8–10) of the dispute about Christians eating food that had been offered in sacrifices to pagan gods. Some at Corinth (called the "strong") saw no problem, on the grounds that these were not gods at all and there was really only one true God. Others (called the "weak") had scruples about participating in idol worship, perhaps based on their former practices before they became Christians. On the intellectual level, Paul agreed with the strong. Nevertheless, on the pastoral, communal level he wanted the strong to respect the consciences of the weak and thus to work out a compromise between them. That meant Paul and the strong putting aside their own views and tailoring their practice out of deference for the weak. In that respect Paul and the strong would be manifesting the self-sacrificing love that Christ showed in his passion and death.

This interpretation of imitation as self-sacrificing love is confirmed by other Pauline texts. For example, in an earlier letter (1 Thessalonians 1:6 and 2:14) Paul used the language of the imitation of him as he commended the Christians for their fidelity in undergoing sufferings on account of the gospel. In his letter to the Philippians, Paul used the description of Christ in an early Christian hymn ("he emptied himself . . . even to death on a cross," 2:7–8) to challenge Christians to humble themselves and pay more attention to the interests of others than to their own interests. And in 2 Corinthians Paul frequently appeals to the character of Jesus — his attitudes and virtues, and especially his self-emptying mode of existence — to describe his own way of discipleship and apostleship, and to challenge the Corinthians to embody a similar kind of discipleship. The imitation of Christ was essential to Paul's discipleship, and it is to ours also.

Bringing the Texts Together

Paul received his call to discipleship on his way to persecute Christians in Damascus. His experience of the risen Christ according to Galatians 1:15–16 not only turned his life around but also left him with the conviction that God had chosen him to bring the good news about Jesus to non-Jews. Paul carried out his call to discipleship as a minister of God's word according to 1 Thessalonians 2:13, which he regarded as an active and creative force whose instrument he considered himself to be. At the same time, Paul developed a loving, personal relationship with those persons to whom he brought the gospel.

In carrying out his calling, Paul faced much opposition on both the personal level (criticism of his appearance and speech) and the theological level (objections to his Law-free gospel for Gentiles). As 2 Corinthians 12:8 shows, Paul learned from experience that his human limitations could make the greatness of the gospel shine forth more brilliantly, because God's "power is made perfect in weakness."

In Romans 15:15–16 Paul describes his ministry as a "priestly service." That is, he viewed bringing his Gentile converts to faith as a gift to God, just as priests in antiquity offered their sacrifices as gifts to God. In shaping the communities he founded, Paul insisted that they be open to all kinds of persons, both slaves like Onesimus and slave owners like Philemon, on the ground that all persons of faith after the pattern of Abraham are one in Christ, equals before God, and thus brothers and sisters (Philemon 15–16).

In challenging his fellow Christians, Paul urged them to "be imitators of me, as I am of Christ" (1 Corinthians 11:1) in the sense of imitating Jesus' self-sacrificing love shown in his passion and death "for us" and "for our sins," and exemplified by Paul in putting aside his own dignity as an apostle and his own opinions in order to smooth the way of discipleship for others.

THINK, PRAY, AND ACT

THINK

1. Read one of the longer descriptions of Paul's conversion/call in Acts 9:22 or 26. Imagine yourself as present. What do you see? What do you hear? What do you feel?
2. Have you experienced the word of God as living and active? When and how?
3. Have you ever experienced God's power made perfect in weakness? When and how?

PRAY

Pray for vocations to the priesthood, sisterhood, and lay ministry.

Read Philippians 2:6–11, and ask God for the grace to imitate the self-sacrificing love displayed by Jesus and Paul.

ACT

Contribute to the financial and/or spiritual support of a missionary working in some remote and difficult situation through your local office of the Propagation of the Faith.

4

Other Ways
of Being a Disciple of Jesus

The theme of discipleship in the New Testament is not confined to the first followers of the earthly Jesus. Indeed when we move beyond the Gospels and Paul's letters and into other parts of the New Testament, we may find some new and fresh perspectives on the theme, meet disciples who in some ways are more like ourselves, and get us thinking better about our own paths of discipleship.

1. Stephen the Martyr

> *"'Look,' he said, 'I see the heavens opened and the Son of Man standing at the right hand of God.'"*
>
> — Acts 7:56

Stephen is often called the "Protomartyr" (or the "first martyr"), since according to the Acts of the Apostles he is the first follower of Jesus after Easter to have died for the public confession of his faith in Jesus. In the church's calendar his feast is celebrated on December 26, a vivid reminder that the joy of Christmas must always be tempered with the sign of the cross.

The story of Stephen is told in Acts 6–7. It is full of fascinating details, which give us precious insights into the early days of the church in Jerusalem. For our purposes, however, the basic point is that Stephen shows us that following Jesus may in some cases lead to the fate that Jesus himself suffered — death by martyrdom.

The word "martyr" derives from the Greek word for "witness." A martyr testifies or bears witness to someone or something. The term has a legal background. In a courtroom a witness/martyr is supposed to provide true and accurate testimony, whatever the consequences may be. The recent phenomenon of Muslim suicide bombers has given martyrdom a bad name. However, the tradition of martyrdom on account of fidelity to one's religious principles — whether they be Christian, Jewish, or Muslim — has a noble heritage that should not be confused with the recent perverse Islamic aberration of killing others to achieve the status of martyr.

According to Acts 6:1–6, Stephen was one of seven men with Greek names appointed to assist the apostles in attending to the material needs of the Christian community at Jerusalem. In particular, they were appointed to make sure that the Greek-speaking ("Hellenist") widows were properly cared for. These women would have been the most needy members of the community. The selection of these men, who are often called "deacons" since they were appointed to assist in serving at table, was supposed to relieve the Twelve Apostles from that task and so free them to work more intensively for the "word of God" or preaching the good news about Jesus.

However, Stephen according to Acts 6:8 immediately launches into a very visible and successful public ministry, without another word about his waiting on table: "Stephen, full of grace and power, did great wonders and signs among the people." His chief opponents seem to have been other Greek-speaking Jews who were from outside the land of Israel but had settled in Jerusalem and frequented "the synagogue of the Freedman." Stephen and the other "deacons" very likely fit the same profile. So did Saul/Paul, who suddenly makes his first appearance in Acts.

It appears that Stephen's opponents took offense at his subordinating the Jerusalem Temple and the Jewish Law to what God had done and was doing through Jesus. For them Stephen's words constituted blasphemy against God and Moses. At issue were the presence of God and the way to carry out God's will. Stephen and his colleagues seemed to say that God is now most present in the community formed around Jesus, and that Jesus was and is the authoritative interpreter of the Jewish Law.

When asked by the Jewish high priest to defend himself, Stephen proceeds to give the longest speech in the Acts of the Apostles, a book famous for its long speeches. The speech in Acts 7:2–53 is a review of ancient Israel's history from Abraham to Stephen's present. It tries to show that "the Most High does not dwell in houses made with human hands" (7:48), and that throughout its history Israel had not kept the Law that it received through angels (7:53). Thus Stephen criticizes the people's reliance on the Jerusalem Temple and the Jewish law for their identity as God's people, and bears witness to his conviction that Jesus has indeed changed "the customs that Moses handed on" (6:14).

At the end of Stephen's witness the high priest disappears, all semblance of a legal proceeding ceases, and the situation degenerates into a mob action and a lynching of Stephen by stoning. The chief "coat holder" turns out to be Saul, who will himself soon undergo a spectacular turnabout from being chief persecutor of the church and become the vehicle by which Stephen's witness is carried on and spread throughout the Mediterranean world. The saying that "the blood of martyrs is the seed of Christians" is already operative in the New Testament.

What makes the account of Stephen's death especially significant for the theme of discipleship is the way in which Stephen dies. Luke the Evangelist seems to have been the author of both the Gospel that bears his name and the Acts of the Apostles. In his two-volume work he develops many parallels between Jesus in the Gospel and his followers in Acts. He also emphasizes the theme of Jesus as a good example, and indeed as the best example of his own teaching. In that sense Jesus too is a martyr, because he dies in perfect harmony with what he taught and practiced during his public ministry.

According to Luke's account of Stephen's martyrdom in Acts 7:54–60, Stephen was filled with the Holy Spirit and was granted a vision of the glory of God and Jesus as the glorious Son of Man. According to Luke 23, the dying Jesus forgives his enemies, promises the "good thief" a place in heaven, and commends his spirit to his heavenly Father. Likewise, at the time of his martyrdom Stephen also makes three statements. He first acknowledges that he sees the heavens opened and "the Son of Man standing at the right hand of God" (7:56). Next he commends his spirit to the risen Jesus, "Lord Jesus, receive my spirit" (7:59). Then he too forgives his enemies, "Lord, do not hold this sin against them" (7:60).

The message that Luke wants to convey by this parallelism is that Stephen the first Christian martyr dies after the pattern set by Jesus the martyr. Both figures are true to their principles and are willing to die for their fidelity to them. The example of Stephen the Protomartyr shows that martyrdom can be a way of following Jesus, a point reaffirmed by thousands and thousands of Christian martyrs throughout the centuries.

2. Philip the Interpreter of Scripture

> *"So Philip ran up to it and heard him reading the prophet Isaiah. He asked, 'Do you understand what you are reading?' He replied, 'How can I unless someone guides me?'"*
>
> — ACTS 8:30–31

While the major figures in Acts are Peter, John, and Paul, we do meet along the way certain other characters such as Philip. Whether he was one of the Twelve Apostles or simply an evangelist who was named Philip has been long debated among scholars. The episode in which Philip features (Acts 8:26–40) shows how a person (in this case an Ethiopian eunuch) can become a disciple through Israel's Scriptures and their proper Christ-centered interpretation.

The story begins when Philip is told to go to the road leading from Jerusalem to Gaza. There he meets up with an Ethiopian eunuch, someone in charge of the queen's treasury, obviously an important person. The word "Ethiopia" here probably refers broadly to Africa to the south of the Holy Land, not necessarily to what we might call Ethiopia today. He had come to Jerusalem to worship and was returning home. Whether we are to regard him as a Jew through heritage or conversion or as a Gentile interested in Judaism, is not clear. In Acts there is a category of persons called "God fearers." They are Gentiles who are attracted to Judaism by its high ethical standards, monotheism, and community life, without however going all the way into Judaism by undergoing circumcision and observing the Sabbath and the laws about ritual and food purity. In either case, the Ethiopian eunuch was interested enough in Judaism to visit the Jerusalem temple and to read the book of Isaiah.

When the angel directs Philip to go to the eunuch's chariot, he finds him reading the passage in the book of Isaiah about the Suffering Servant, and in particular Isaiah 53:7–8. There someone is described as being like a lamb led to the slaughter and as put to death unjustly. The eunuch wants to know who this figure was.

This passage comes from the part of the book of Isaiah (chapters 40–55) known as Second Isaiah, which was composed during the Babylonian exile in the sixth century B.C. At several points in that section a mysterious figure called the "Servant of the LORD" appears. Scholars today still argue about his identity. Some regard him as a specific historical figure such as the legitimate king of Judah, a prophet within the community, or some other leader. Others view him as a symbolic figure representing all Israel, the exiled community, or a group within it.

While the identity of the sixth-century Servant may not be clear, his profile in Isaiah 52:13–53:12 is clear. First in 52:13–15 God promises that his Servant will prosper, despite the fact that his appearance has been so marred by suffering that he barely seems human at all. Then in 53:1–10 the "many" also express their amazement at his appearance but find in him and his sufferings expiation or atonement for their sins: "He was wounded for our transgressions, crushed for our iniquities, upon him was the punishment that made us whole, and by his bruises we are healed" (Isaiah 53:5). It is in this context that he is described as being like a lamb led to the slaughter.

And finally in 53:11–12 God promises to vindicate his Servant precisely because "he bore the sins of many, and made intercession for the transgressors."

The Ethiopian eunuch wants to know who exactly this Servant of the Lord is who is being described in such detail in the book of Isaiah. He recognizes that on his own he cannot find the answer to his question. So when Philip appears, he asks for guidance in his reading. Philip, of course, identifies the Servant as Jesus of Nazareth and proceeds to tell him the "good news" about Jesus.

What Philip offers the Ethiopian is a Christ-centered, or Christological, reading of the Old Testament. Early Christians devoted much time and energy to showing how many mysterious texts in the Old Testament had suddenly become clear to them when interpreted with reference to the life, death, and resurrection of Jesus. And one of their favorite texts was Isaiah 52:13–53:12.

This kind of "actualizing" interpretation of Scripture was common among Jews in New Testament times. For example, among the Dead Sea scrolls there were found a number of texts called "Pesharim." These works look like biblical commentaries, consisting of the quotations of biblical texts and interpretations of them. Most of the Pesharim are devoted to the interpretation of Psalms and prophetic texts, and especially to passages whose historical contexts had been lost and now seemed more like riddles or puzzles than the word of God. So the Jews who produced these commentaries interpreted those texts in terms of the history and life of their own Jewish movement (most likely Essenism). Behind their activity was the insight that "the word of God is living and active, sharper than any two-edged sword" (Hebrews 4:12).

The New Testament is full of "actualizing," Christ-centered biblical interpretations of Scripture. The phrase "according to the Scriptures" is quite common. So persuaded was the Ethiopian eunuch by Philip's interpretation of Isaiah 53:7–8 that he demanded to be baptized immediately. And Philip complied with his request. Now the Ethiopian had the key to understanding the Scriptures of Israel. That key was the person of Jesus. He alone opened up all those puzzling and mysterious texts. He was the Servant of the Lord, despised and beaten for us and for our sins, and vindicated by God in his resurrection from the dead and now able to bring about right relationship with God and eternal life with God. The Ethiopian became a disciple of Jesus through reading the Scriptures of Israel and their Christ-centered interpretation by Philip.

3. Timothy the Church Leader

> *"Let no one despise your youth, but set the believers an example in speech and conduct, in love, in faith, in purity."*
>
> — 1 TIMOTHY 4:12

Timothy is a major figure in Paul's letters and in those parts of Acts devoted to Paul's apostolic activity. His name appears alongside Paul's in the salutation of several Pauline letters, and he serves as Paul's trusted associate and emissary in many difficult situations. Two of the so-called Pastoral Epistles are addressed directly to Timothy. While in 2 Timothy the apostle Paul is facing death and so offers his farewell or testament, in 1 Timothy Paul provides advice about constructing a stable Christian community. Our focus here is not so much on the origin of the Pastoral Epistles or on Timothy's biography as it is on what Paul is asking Timothy to do as a church administrator. This too was an important way of being a disciple according to the New Testament.

In 1 Timothy Paul is asking Timothy to remain in Ephesus (on the west coast of present-day Turkey) and ensure that the local Christian community there settle down for the long haul and achieve some measure of stability. As an apostle, Paul journeyed from place to place, founding churches and moving on when a certain basic level of stability had been reached. But as 1 Corinthians and other letters show, much work remained to be done before the local church was able to reach spiritual and structural maturity and find equilibrium with the world around it.

In 1 Timothy Paul is commissioning Timothy to serve as his "apostolic delegate" in Ephesus. Likewise, in his letter to Titus he commissions Titus to serve as his apostolic delegate on the island of Crete. In both cases Paul's representative is supposed to oversee the further organization and functioning of the local Christian community. He is not the bishop (which means "overseer"). In fact, he is to find local persons who might serve as bishops and deacons, thus insuring greater stability in the community at large. The purpose of the letter known as 1 Timothy and the letter to Titus is to give Paul's advice on how to achieve this goal.

According to the letter addressed to him, Timothy is expected to do six things: ensure sound doctrine, establish right order in worship, find appropriate local leaders to serve as bishops and deacons, care for the needy, encourage external social respectability, and provide a good example for others. Attention to Paul's instructions to Timothy in 1 Timothy can open up still another New Testament way of discipleship, a way that is especially relevant for those engaged in enriching and building up the local church.

Ensure sound doctrine. After the usual greetings, Paul emphasizes the importance of Timothy insisting on sound doctrine, that is, what stands in line with Paul's own proclamation of the gospel. The positive ideal is neatly expressed in 1 Timothy 1:5 as "love that comes from a pure heart, a good conscience, and sincere faith." At several points Paul suggests that there had been problems caused by what he regarded as false doctrine: the "meaningless talk" from alleged teachers of the law (1:6–7), the moral "shipwreck" caused by Hymenaeus and Alexander (1:19–20), and the false asceticism that forbade marriage and demanded abstinence from certain foods (4:3). To counter these deviations, Paul sprinkles the letter with short summaries of the gospel (see 1:15; 2:5–6; 3:16) which surely reflect the faith of Paul and his converts and thus represent the authentic "deposit of faith."

Establish order in worship. In 1 Corinthians 11–14 Paul showed himself to be very concerned about disorder at worship in the Christian community. Likewise in 1 Timothy he urges that in the Christian assembly there should be prayers for all sorts of persons, including kings and others in high positions. He also insists that the men should pray peaceably, that women should be modestly dressed, and that women should learn from their husbands rather than exercising authority over men in public. This kind of order within the community clearly reflects a desire for external respectability and conformity to the social norms of the larger Greco-Roman society.

Find appropriate local leaders. In 3:1–13 Paul provides lists of qualifications for those who might aspire to the offices of bishop and deacon. He describes the office of bishop as a "noble task." That apparently was not self-evident to the letter's first readers. Rather, one of Timothy's duties was to make these offices more attractive and important in the local community. According to 3:1–7 the bishop must be a model of external respectability (not a drunkard or a lover of money), be able to manage his own household well, should not be a recent convert (lest he drift away), and ought to be well regarded by outsiders. Nothing is said about knowledge or faith. Likewise the deacon must be well respected within and outside the community, and known for piety and a clear conscience. According to 3:11 it appears that women were also eligible to serve as deacons: "Women likewise must be serious, not slanderers, but temperate, faithful in all things." Later in the letter (5:17–22) there are provisions for the office of elder or presbyter. How exactly this office fit in with those of bishop and deacon is hard to grasp from the text, though eventually the hierarchy of bishop, presbyter/priest, and deacon became the norm.

Care for the needy. First Timothy 5:3–16 makes provisions for the local community to care for the neediest and most defenseless category of persons in the ancient social order — widows. It envisions a kind of "order" of widows supported by other church members, with the expectation that the widows will pray for the needs of the church. A good deal of attention is given to determining who is a real widow and thus who qualifies for community support. A true widow must be over sixty years of age, married only once, and having a reputation for good works.

Encourage external respectability. The Pastoral Epistles reflect a period in which the church is settling down in the Greco-Roman world and achieving a certain equilibrium or compromise with the world around it. It is still very much a minority movement. Its most effective missionary strategy is the good example of its members. Therefore Timothy is urged to encourage not only the church officers but all its members to cultivate the virtues of prudence, justice, temperance, and fortitude, along with piety. The hope is that the respectability of ordinary Christians will attract others to their faith and fellowship.

Provide a good example for others. In 4:11–16 Paul urges Timothy to offer a good example in his pattern of life and in his spiritual leadership of the church at Ephesus: "Give attention to the public reading of scripture, to exhorting, to teaching." And in 6:11–16 he directs Timothy to "pursue righteousness, godliness, faith, love, endurance, gentleness," and challenges him to fight the good fight of the faith" and "take hold of the eternal life to which you were called." The church leader must work as hard (or even harder) as any other Christian walking the way of discipleship.

4. Discouraged Disciples in Hebrews and 1 Peter

> *"Let us hold fast to the confession of our hope without wavering, for he who has promised is faithful."*
>
> — Hebrews 10:23

Two of the most theologically rich texts in the New Testament are Hebrews and 1 Peter. Both are exhortations or sermons addressed to discouraged disciples and expressed in letter form. Both presuppose a social setting in which Christians are a minority and run the risk of being swallowed up in the surrounding society. Both speak to Christians who seem discouraged in their faith and stand in need of a word of encouragement or consolation. Both seek to help discouraged disciples by appealing to Christ — the High Priest in Hebrews, and the Suffering Servant in 1 Peter.

The recipients of the letter to the Hebrews seem to have been Jewish Christians. They may well have lived in Rome around A.D. 70. They presumably would have known the Jewish Scriptures well enough to follow and appreciate the many biblical references made in the course of the author's argument. And they seem to be anticipating or undergoing some kind of persecution as well as internal discouragement with their new faith in Christ.

We learn more about their concrete situation only near the end of the work, with its many calls for the audience to persevere in faith. The author notes that "many are neglecting to meet together" (10:25), and reminds them of their struggles with suffering in the past, "sometimes being publicly exposed to abuse and persecution, and sometimes being partners with those so treated" (10:33). He also recalls their compassion for those in prison and their patient acceptance of the plundering of their possessions (10:34). However, in 12:4 he observes that "in your struggle against sin you have not yet resisted to the point of shedding blood," thus indicating that the current persecution was not yet widespread. They also seem in danger of returning to the kind of Judaism into which they were born. There they would find a larger community in Rome, and might profit from the political understanding that had developed between Romans and Jews that gave Jews certain rights and privileges.

The author's response was to show that Christ is the key to the Jewish Scriptures (1:1–4:13), and that Christ represents a better way to worship God than the rites connected with the Levitical priesthood allowed (4:14–10:18). With reference to the Jewish Scriptures, the author shows that Christ is superior to the angels and to Moses, that he is the "Son of Man" prophesied in Psalm 8, and that he alone can give the "Sabbath" rest promised to God's people in Psalm 95.

With reference to the priesthood of Christ he shows how Christ fits the definition of the compassionate high priest, that his priesthood is rooted not in the order of Levi but rather in the earlier and better order of Melchizedek, and that he represents a better covenant and a better priesthood. The fundamental theological insight of Hebrews is that Jesus is both the perfect (in the sense of truly effective) sacrifice for sins and the great high priest (because he offered himself willingly for the sins of humankind). The idea seems to be that the best medicine for discouraged disciples is to remind them of what God has done for them in Christ and who they have become as a result.

The recipients of 1 Peter seem to have been Gentile Christians living in several communities in north-central Asia Minor (present-day Turkey). The letter was intended to be circulated from community to community, and thus can be called an encyclical. It came from "Peter" and the church in "Babylon," probably code for Rome. It offers advice to suffering and discouraged Christians, links their present sufferings to those of Christ the Servant of God, and urges them to remember their new identity as members of the holy people of God.

The sufferings undergone by these Christians seem to have been more along the line of social ostracism than active governmental persecution. They were new Christians, and their conversion from ignorance and futile ways (1:14, 18) meant a split from their former ways of acting and their former friends and relatives: "They are surprised that you no longer join them in the same excesses of dissipation, and so they blaspheme" (4:4).

Their new efforts at Christian discipleship led them to regard themselves to be members of something wonderfully new — the biblical people of God, and yet also somewhat alienated and estranged in the world around them. In 2:11 they are even addressed as "aliens and exiles." Whether this refers to their spiritual alienation or reflects their socioeconomic status as migrant workers, is debated among scholars. What is clear is that they have found in the church "a home for the homeless."

In exhorting and encouraging these discouraged disciples, Peter emphasizes the new identity they have received through their incorporation into Christ through baptism. He also addresses them in terms used in the Jewish Scriptures to describe Israel at Mount Sinai, "You are a chosen race, a royal priesthood, a holy nation, God's own people" (2:9; see Exodus 19). In essence, they are no longer "Gentiles," because through Jesus Christ they have received divine mercy and become part of God's people. That is the identity that they should hang on to and take pride in.

What can help them deal with their sufferings and discouragements is reflection on the sufferings of Christ and their effects. Early on (1:18–19) Peter speaks of their having been ransomed from their futile ways by the precious blood of Christ. In 3:21–24 he points them to the good example of Christ the Suffering Servant ("He committed no sin, and no deceit was found in his mouth," see Isaiah 53:9). He goes further to remind them that the sufferings of Christ had the positive effect of making possible the new relationship with God that they were now enjoying: "He himself bore our sins in his body on the cross, so that, free from sins, we might live for righteousness; by his wounds you have been healed" (see Isaiah 53:5).

What Thomas G. Long wrote (in *Hebrews,* 1997, pp. 3–5) about the author of Hebrews applies equally well to the author of 1 Peter. Both authors were convinced that the state of spiritual weariness present in their addressees was best met by Christology and preaching. They were convinced that the solution was not improved group dynamics, better conflict management techniques, or more lively liturgies (however valuable these may be) but rather reflection on the theological significance of Jesus' death and resurrection. Both were bold enough to preach in complex theological terms about the nature and meaning of Jesus Christ. That is what they regarded as the best antidote to spiritual discouragement among the followers of Jesus.

5. James the Sage

> *"If any of you is lacking in wisdom, ask God, who gives to all generously and ungrudgingly, and it will be given you."*
>
> — JAMES 1:5

Still another way of being a disciple of Jesus according to the New Testament is to become a sage, a person of wisdom. What is known commonly as the letter of James is in fact a wisdom instruction. It mentions Jesus only twice, both times in a formulaic way as the "Lord Jesus Christ" (1:1; 2:1). This is, of course, a very elevated title, since it identifies Jesus as the "Messiah" ("Christ") and as divine ("Lord"). However, there is no development of the significance of the various elements in it. There are many wisdom sayings in the letter that echo sayings of Jesus in the Gospels; for example, about not swearing oaths (James 5:12 = Matthew 5:33–37). But there is no attribution of them to Jesus. The lack of explicit interest in the person of Jesus led Martin Luther to describe it as "the epistle of straw" and to banish it to the far reaches of the biblical canon of Scripture.

The wisdom instruction is cast in the form of a letter from "James, a servant of God and of the Lord Jesus Christ" to "the twelve tribes in the Dispersion." While there are several persons named James (or Jacob) in the New Testament, we are most likely meant to identify this author with James "the brother of the Lord" (see Galatians 1:19). Whether this James was a full sibling of Jesus (not possible according to Catholic tradition, since Mary is ever-virgin), a half-brother, or some other kind of relative has been debated for many centuries. But we need not solve that problem here. The audience seems to be Jewish Christians living outside the land of Israel (the Dispersion).

In form and content much in the letter of James sounds like material found in parts of the books of Proverbs and Sirach (Ecclesiasticus). Its teachings are clearly the result of serious reflection on real-life situations and efforts to encapsulate human experience in a concise and memorable manner. It is a wisdom instruction.

James is most famous for his apparent criticism of Paul's teaching on justification by faith in 2:14–26. Whether James had Paul himself in mind or some extreme version of Paul's teaching, his point is that faith without works is dead. It is easy enough to claim to have faith. But faith without works is barren. James even argues that in his willingness to sacrifice Isaac (see Genesis 22), Abraham himself was justified by his works. James insists that "a person is justified by works and not by faith alone" (2:25). No wonder Luther disliked the letter of James. (The dispute may not be as sharp as it seems if we take account of Paul's own ideal of "faith working through love" in Galatians 5:6.)

Despite its theological limitations, the letter of James contains many wise and important teachings. It insists that we be doers of the word and not hearers only (1:22). It defines true religion as "to care for orphans and widows in their distress, and to keep oneself unstained by the world" (1:27). It criticizes any semblance of partiality in the Christian assembly and urges that rich and poor be treated as equals (2:1–7). It reflects on the harm that "loose" tongues can do in purveying gossip and slander (3:1–12). It traces conflicts and wars to desires to take the possessions and property of others (4:1–12). It makes scathing criticisms of rich and greedy persons (4:13–5:6). It urges patient waiting for the day of the Lord, denounces careless oaths and vows, commends the anointing of the sick and confession of sins in the assembly, and praises those who seek out those who have strayed from the Christian community.

The letter of James illustrates still another New Testament way of being a disciple of Jesus, even without much explicit focus on him. While it may not be one of the core documents of the New Testament, it does convey much sound and practical wisdom, and so enriches the Christian canon of Scripture by its presence, and enriches the theme of discipleship.

6. John the Visionary

"I was in the spirit on the Lord's day."

— REVELATION 1:10

The author of the book of Revelation illustrates still another New Testament way of being a disciple of Jesus: the visionary. The author's name was John, a common name (with various forms) among Jews in the first century. He was very likely not the same as the author of John's Gospel or of the three letters of John. According to his own testimony, he was on the island of Patmos, off the western coast of Asia Minor (present-day Turkey). He was thoroughly conversant with the state of the various churches in western Asia Minor. He seems to have been an evangelist/teacher, and he describes his exile on Patmos as "because of the word of God and the testimony of Jesus" (Revelation 1:9).

John was a Jewish Christian. He knew the Jewish Scriptures inside out, and almost every verse in his book contains an allusion to or an echo of Scripture. However, he never quotes the biblical texts directly and often changes their contexts and meanings rather radically. Thus he uses Scripture to express his ideas but at the same time respects the new things God has done in and through Jesus. He appears to be alienated from other Jewish groups in the area, and even refers to them as constituting "the synagogue of Satan" (2:9). He is also familiar with the form of Judaism known as apocalyptic.

The term "apocalyptic" derives from the Greek word for "revelation." Thus John's book is known alternatively as the Apocalypse or the book of Revelation. An apocalypse is strictly speaking a literary form. It is a narrative in which a visionary or dreamer recounts his experience of visiting the heavenly realm and/or describes the future course of history. Though based on Scripture, the imagery tends to be very colorful and even to assault the senses with its richness. As a result, the adjective "apocalyptic" is also used more loosely to describe the content of such writings: the heavenly realm or future history. The Jewish apocalypses include parts of the book of Daniel, 1 Enoch, 4 Ezra (= 2 Esdras 3–14), and 2 Baruch. And apocalyptic thinking has influenced many of the Dead Sea scrolls, as well as large parts of the New Testament (especially John's Gospel and Paul's letters).

John begins his apocalypse by reporting in 1:9–20 the vision of the risen Jesus that he experienced on Patmos on "the Lord's Day" (presumably Sunday). He is first told to write in a book what he sees and to send it to the seven churches in western Asia Minor. Next he sees the glorious risen Jesus and describes his features in words and images based on various biblical texts. Then he hears the risen Jesus identify himself in terms of his resurrection: "I am the first and the last, and the living one. I was dead, and see, I am alive forever and ever; and I have the keys of Death and of Hades" (1:17–18). By his resurrection Christ has conquered death and now has power over life and death.

The occasion for John's book seems to have been a persecution (or the threat of one) of Christians in the area of seven churches. This becomes relatively clear in what is the central vision of the book in chapters 12–14. In Revelation 12 John has a vision of the Mother of the Messiah and the birth of her son threatened by the Great Red Dragon. Then he views a battle in the heavens whereby the Dragon (who is Satan) is thrown out of the heavenly court but allowed temporarily to persecute the church on earth. In chapter 13 he has a further vision of the "Beast from the Sea" (the Roman emperor) and the cult surrounding him as if he were a god. Then he sees the "Beast from the Land" (a local political and/or religious official) who is promoting the worship of the emperor and persecutes those (like the Christians) who refuse to accept the emperor as "Lord and God." These three figures constitute a kind of "unholy trinity" in opposition to the church. But their power is only temporary. In chapter 14 John has visions of the triumph of the Lamb (the risen Jesus) and the martyrs over the forces of evil. The message to those facing persecution is, Hold on! Be patient! The war has been won through Jesus' death and resurrection. The present battle is only for a short time. And so remain faithful!

The crisis facing the Christians addressed in the book of Revelation involved their being forced to participate in worshipping the Roman emperor as a god. For those like John, doing so would compromise their primary identity as Christians. For him, the risen Jesus is the only "Lord and God," and to grant those titles to the emperor was blasphemy. And so he wrote down his visions especially to encourage wavering Christians to remain firm in their faith and to resist even to the point of martyrdom the pressures being applied by the local official on them to participate in the public worship of the emperor as a god.

John's visions proceed largely in terms of the number seven, a "perfect" number of sorts. So there are letters to seven churches in chapters 2 to 3, followed by the visions of the seven seals in 6:12–8:1, the seven trumpets in 8:2–11:19, the seven bowls in 15:1–16:21, and the seven great end-time events in 19:11–21:8. Also included are John's initial vision of the heavenly court in 4:1–5:14, his vision of the fall of Babylon (= Rome) in 17:1–19:10, and the climactic vision of the New Jerusalem in 21:9–22:5. There is in these visions a good deal for repetition, and many of the units could easily stand on their own.

Revelation is the book of the risen Christ, in that it takes its inspiration from John's initial vision of the risen Christ. It is also very much a book of hope. Although the present situation of persecution (or the threat of it) seemed terrifying, John's visions of the risen Christ and his triumph over the forces of death and evil provided the words and images that helped suffering Christians see things in the proper perspective of their faith and endure whatever came their way. Through his own experiences, John on Patmos showed that being a visionary can also be a way of Christian discipleship.

Bringing the Texts Together

The various figures treated in this chapter show that there are many ways of being disciples of the risen Jesus. The example of Stephen in Acts 6–7 shows that under extreme conditions following Jesus may end in martyrdom as it did for Jesus himself. Philip in Acts 8 exercises his discipleship by interpreting the Scriptures (especially Isaiah 53) in terms of their fulfillment through Jesus.

Close attention to Paul's directives in 1 Timothy shows how important church leadership and administration can be for setting local Christian communities on the right path. The "discouraged disciples" addressed in Hebrews and 1 Peter seem to have been on the verge of giving up on their Christian discipleship, and so both writers sought to revitalize their faith by pointing to Jesus as the High Priest and Suffering Servant, respectively.

Despite the little explicit mention of Jesus, the letter of James indicates that being a sage — one who is wise about both human nature and the workings of the Christian community — is yet another way of being a disciple. Finally John the visionary reminds us how important it can be in times of crisis or danger to focus again on the risen Christ and there find hope from his victory over sin and death.

THINK, PRAY, AND ACT

THINK

1. Do you ever feel discouraged with your own efforts at discipleship? What gets you down the most?
2. With which mode of discipleship treated in this chapter — martyr, Scripture teacher, church leader, sage, or visionary — do you identify most closely?
3. Is there another category that better describes your own efforts at discipleship? What is it?

PRAY

Read Revelation 1:9–20 slowly and meditatively, and imagine yourself as John the visionary. What do you hear? What do you see?

Ask God for the grace to see your own path of discipleship more clearly.

ACT

Seek out a valued friend or spiritual guide, and reflect together on how you might better understand your own way of discipleship and how you might better use your gifts for others and for the church.

Conclusion

Ten Points on Discipleship

The main point of this book has been to show the rich diversity in the New Testament theme of following Jesus. However, it is also possible to cull from the many texts analyzed here ten general points about discipleship.

1. The context of Christian discipleship is the kingdom of God in its present and future dimensions and the good news (gospel) about Jesus' life, death, and resurrection.

2. The call to discipleship may be abrupt (as in the Synoptic Gospels and in the case of Paul) or gradual (as in John's Gospel).

3. There are different ways of responding to and acting upon the call to discipleship.

4. The call to discipleship involves being with Jesus and extending his mission of teaching and healing/reconciling.

5. Answering the call requires trust and hope in God's promises made in and through Jesus.

6. The prospective disciple needs to count the cost and reckon with the possibility (and even probability) of opposition and suffering.

7. The prospective disciple must let go of what might be obstacles to discipleship (riches, status, attachments, etc.) and the fears that might accompany following Jesus' call.

8. The disciple must be willing to bear witness to Jesus in word and deed.

9. Answering the call outweighs other obligations, commitments, and relationships.

10. Jesus promises rewards not only in the present (the hundredfold in the new family of Jesus) but also in the future (eternal life).

For Further Reading

Barton, Stephen C. *Discipleship and Family Ties in Mark and Matthew.* Cambridge, UK: Cambridge University Press, 1994.

Beirne, Margaret. *Women and Men in the Fourth Gospel: A Discipleship of Equals.* London and New York: Sheffield Academic Press, 2003.

Best, Ernest. *Following Jesus: Discipleship in the Gospel of Mark.* Sheffield, UK: JSOT Press, 1981.

Bonhoeffer, Dietrich. *The Cost of Discipleship.* New York: Simon and Schuster, 1995.

Chennattu, Rekha. *Johannine Discipleship as a Covenant Relationship.* Peabody, MA: Hendrickson, 2006.

Donahue, John R. *The Theology and Setting of Discipleship in the Gospel of Mark.* Milwaukee: Marquette University Press, 1983.

Fischer, Georg, and Martin Hasitschka. *The Call of the Disciple: The Bible on Following Christ.* New York: Paulist, 1999.

Harrington, Daniel J., and James F. Keenan. *Jesus and Virtue Ethics.* Lanham, MD: Rowman and Littlefield, 2002.

Harrington, Daniel J., and James F. Keenan. *Paul and Virtue Ethics.* Lanham, MD: Rowman and Littlefield, 2010.

Henderson, Suzanne Watts. *Christology and Discipleship in the Gospel of Mark.* Cambridge, UK: Cambridge University Press, 2006.

Hengel, Martin. *The Charismatic Leader and His Followers.* Edinburgh: T&T Clark, 1996.

Longenecker, Richard N. (ed.). *Patterns of Discipleship in the New Testament.* Grand Rapids: Eerdmans, 1996.

Segovia, Fernando F. (ed.) *Discipleship in the New Testament.* Philadelphia: Fortress, 1985.

Stock, Augustine. *Counting the Cost: New Testament Teaching on Discipleship.* Collegeville: Liturgical Press, 1977.

Sweetland, Dennis M. *Our Journey with Jesus: Discipleship According to Luke-Acts.* Collegeville: Liturgical Press, 1990.

Sweetland, Dennis M. *Our Journey with Jesus: Discipleship According to Mark.* Wilmington, DE: Michael Glazier, 1987.

Wilkins, Michael. *Discipleship in the Ancient World and Matthew's Gospel.* Grand Rapids: Baker, 1995.